Ulrich Enzel

Algarve

Translated by Tom Krupp

51 selected walks
on the southern and western coasts as well as the hinterland of the
Algarve

With 80 colour photographs,
51 walking maps with a scale of 1:50,000 / 1:100,000 and
2 overview maps with a scale of 1:750,000 / 1:1,500,000

ROTHER · MUNICH

Cover photo:
The cave coast of Benagil
Photo: Ulrich Montigel.

Frontispiece (page 2):
In the Barlavento: Cliffs by Armação de Pêra

All photographs are by Ulrich Enzel und Ulrich Montigel.

Cartography:
Walking maps with a scale of 1:50,000 / 1:100,000 © Bergverlag Rother
GmbH, Munich (drawn by Gerhard Tourneau, Munich). Overview maps
with a scale of 1:750,000 and 1:1,500,000 © Freytag & Berndt, Vienna

Translation:
Tom Krupp

1st edition 2005
© Bergverlag Rother GmbH, Munich

ISBN 3-7633-4825-5

Distributed in Great Britain by Cordee, 3a De Montfort Street, Leicester
Great Britain LE1 7HD, www.cordee.co.uk

ROTHER WALKING GUIDES

Algarve · Andalucía South · Azores · Bernese Oberland East · Corsica · Côte d'Azur · Crete East · Crete West ·
Cyprus · Gomera · Gran Canaria · Iceland · La Palma · Madeira · Mallorca · Mont Blanc · Norway South ·
Provence · Pyrenees 1 · Pyrenees 2 · Pyrenees 3 · Sardinia · Sicily · High Tatra · Tenerife · Tuscany North ·
Valais East · Valais West · Around the Zugspitze

**Dear mountain lovers! We would be happy to hear your opinion and
suggestions for amendment to this Rother walking guide.**

BERGVERLAG ROTHER · Munich
D-85521 Ottobrunn · Haidgraben 3 · Tel. (089) 608669-0, Fax -69
Internet www.rother.de · **E-mail** bergverlag@rother.de

Preface

The Algarve! Those who frequent the south-westernmost corner of the European continent have a vivid picture of the scenery here. The Algarve – conjures up a steep coastline always new and surprising in its various configurations of sandstone cliffs in colours ranging from yellow through red. The Algarve – endless stretches of idyllic white sand beach with countless bays perfect for bathing. The Algarve – a crystal-clear ocean, ideal for swimming, diving or surfing, a long season of sunshine with a fresh and pleasant sea breeze off the Atlantic, the warm hospitality and a cuisine based on Europe's best coastal fishing grounds. It's the truth: the Algarve lives up to the promises of brochures and documentaries. Beach life at its very best! A fabulous holiday is guaranteed.

Then why go walking? What is the purpose of this guide? Does the Algarve have even more to offer? Indeed, this stretch of land blessed eternally by its weather, with a mountain chain not only climatically separating the rest of Portugal to the north, is made up of more than just coastline and beaches. The hilly countryside rising to heights approaching the 1000 m mark as it elevates northward, the rocky coast facing the open Atlantic to the west and the rarely-visited Sotavento region to the east offer extra gems from this landmass on the far edge of Europe.

This guide intends to encourage excursions into the unknown. Walking in the Barlavento, the »classic« Algarve coastal region west of Faro should help inspire walkers to become acquainted with other stretches of beach apart from that beautiful bay lying directly in front of their hotels. Expansive, fairly unfrequented tracts of coastline are still there to discover. Only a few kilometres away from the bustling, tourist seaside a fantastically diverse geological and botanical landscape unfolds. From the first flowers in spring until autumn's harvest, walking the hinterland offers a multitude of charms. Also, in the hot summer months, the walker searching for shade will find cool relief in the forests of the Monchique hills – and enjoy fantastic views as well. The untamed coastal region to the west and the peaceful realm of the Sotavento to the east nicely round off this diversity.

All of the routes have been walked recently to insure the most reliable information possible. Recent events ranging from newly-laid trails to forest fires can block former trails or provide additional ones. For this reason, please contact the publisher if you discover changes or encounter problems when following a route description. We, and other walkers using the guide, would be most thankful.

Above all, I wish you many lovely, relaxing and eventful days while walking in the Algarve.

December 2004   Dr. Ulrich Enzel

Contents

Tourist Information

Use of the Guide

The guide is divided into five walking regions, described individually in an introductory preface. All of the cited destination and starting points as well as the localities are listed in the index. The map on the back cover provides an overview of the locations of the individual walks.

First, the most important information for each of the recommended walks is summarised under a list of key points. In addition, the individual routes are marked on the coloured overview map for the walk.

Grade

Although seldom marked or signposted, most of the walks follow distinct trails and paths, with only moderate ascents and descents. Some of the walks require a good sense of direction and a certain amount of physical fitness. The walk descriptions provide details of possibly strenuous and/or exposed stretches as well as those requiring a good head for heights. To help judge the difficulty of the suggested walks more easily, the route numbers are colour-coded as follows:

BLUE

These walks follow trails which are generally wide, only moderately steep and relatively harmless even during periods of poor weather.

RED

These walks follow mostly wide trails and the route is easy to follow for the experienced walker with a developed sense of direction. Due to steeper ascents and descents, these walks require a certain degree of physical fitness.

Dangers

Weather conditions in the Algarve are usually very stable, nevertheless, it is recommended to keep an eye on the weather forecast especially when planning longer walks in the countryside or in the Monchique hills. Steady rains can turn a path into a fast-flowing stream and a stream into a river that is difficult to cross.

On the Algarve coast, the difference in sea level during low and high tides can be up to 4 m. You should pick up the current tide table at the hotel reception desk or at the local tourist office. On a beach walk, be well aware of the fact that many stretches are only accessible about 3 hours before and after a low tide. During high tide, cliffs that are difficult to climb are often the only alternative to getting wet or worse.

Hunting season takes place from August 15 to February 27 but only on Thursdays, Sundays and holidays. Walks in the Algarve countryside should particularly be avoided on these days.

Snakes are more often encountered in the summer or autumn, some are even poisonous (e.g. the common viper) and reach lengths of 2 m. You should never walk barefoot or in sandals. Snakes typically nestle in walls and in wet areas. Scorpions are found mostly in summer and tend to seek out shady spots. If you take off your shoes during a break, you'd better check before putting them back on! Scorpions can also be encountered under boulders or rocks. Stings are painful but not serious. The bark of a free-roving dog can be quite loud but they are usually harmless and may even provide a welcome companion. If you feel threatened, picking up a stone or acting out a throw is usually enough to chase the intruder away.

Best times of the year

In the Algarve, the walking season begins already in January due to the attraction of the almond trees in blossom – »Algarve snow« – which flower until the beginning of March, and also because of usually mild weather. March through May and September and October are the best months for walking, thanks to moderate temperatures and little rainfall. During the summer expect intense heat. Starting at the end of October, short but heavy showers may well occur, triggering a »second spring« greening and blooming but at the same time turning many trails into muddy tracks.

The west – at the Praia da Ingrina.

Equipment

Aside from the few walks along sand beaches, most routes require sturdy shoes with non-slip soles. Durable, full-length trousers (protection from *phrygana* vegetation and snakes), protective gear for wind, rain and against the cold, head covering for sun and/or rain and possibly swimming gear are required for most walks. Sufficient liquids and hiking provisions should be taken along, as well as an effective sunscreen lotion.

Maps

The walking maps provided in the guide generally suffice as the best aid for orientation during the walks. For planning the approach to the starting point as well as returning from the destination, we recommend the road and walking map »Algarve« with a scale of 1:150,000 from Freytag & Berndt.

Long-distance wanderlust – near Burgau.

Walking Times
The times indicated only represent the actual walking times – not including breaks for resting, swimming or taking photographs. In the case of long-distance walks, the times for the individual stages are also cited.

Food and Accommodation
Not counting the stretch along the coast developed for tourism, numerous additional accommodations can be found as well. These are mentioned in the prefaces to the individual walking regions. Detailed information regarding dining and refreshment can be found in the descriptions of the individual walks.

Approach
Each walk description contains exact details concerning approach routes when using public or private transport. Current bus and train schedules can be called up under www.eva-transportes.pt. A private vehicle is required to reach some trailheads. Especially when more people are involved, taxis are a fairly inexpensive alternative. Car hire is readily available at the airport as well as in all tourist centres.

Tips for linear and long-distance walkers
Many of the routes suggested here are conceived as linear walks. Since the destination is often far from the starting point, it is recommended that the return be made by public transport (bus or a taxi booked in advance).

Another possibility is to make arrangements with another walker/driver for the walk; one car should be parked at the starting point and the other at the destination, then the walk could be undertaken together or car keys swapped when meeting up along the way for the drive back using the other walker's car.

Long-distance walkers will find the fully-described coastal walks from Sagres to Faro and from Ilha da Culatra to Monte Gordo attractive. The routes in the Monchique hills can also be combined as well as those in the region around Alte and Salir. Due to the extensive farming in the Algarve hinterland, this area is truly »a land of a thousand trails«! Those described in this guide comprise only a small selection.

Nature and environmental protection
Do not make open fires, especially during the dry summer months and do not carelessly throw away cigarette ends – forest and brush fires are not uncommon. Please respect all plants and animals and avoid disturbing them. Take all your litter back with you.

When passing through gates, remember to leave them open or closed as you found them. Please conserve water – due to the increasing number of tourists and despite the seeming abundance of water, even the Algarve suffers from water shortages.

Walking in the Algarve

The Algarve – a unique part of Portugal

Since time immemorial, the Algarve, this south-westernmost chunk of Europe, has lain »over the hills and far away«. This expression applies both geographically and climatically: the Serra de Monchique and Serra do Caldeirão, mountain chains reaching up to 1000 m, separate the Algarve from Alentejo and from all the other northern provinces of Portugal. With an area of 4960 sq km, this makes up only 1/20 of Portugal's total landmass but an incredible variety of natural landscapes are arranged here in this topsy-turvy rectangle measuring 135 km in length between the Atlantic and the Guadiana River and 27 to 50 km in breadth. Out of a population of 350,000, 10 % live in the regional capital of Faro. The coastal area between Luz and Tavira is densely populated as well. In the north-east, beyond Salir however, walkers can go long distances without meeting a soul.

Not many decades have passed since farming and fishing were the economic pillars of the region. The big boom began when North European »snowbirds« discovered the Algarve coastlines. Since then, not quite 100,000 beds in hotel accommodation are offered – half of the total available in all of Portugal. This led to a massive desertion of the agricultural community resulting in many of the typical small-time farms now lying fallow. Only in the environs of Faro and in Sotavento can large-scale enterprises specialising in vegetable farming be found. Fortunately, almond trees continue to bloom so the country lanes are maintained as well as many of the villages and hamlets; the walker can enjoy the hilly countryside along a good network of trails.

Every visitor is acquainted with the sandstone cliffs of the Barlavento, the western coast of the Algarve, at least through tourist brochures. The diversity found on this stretch of coast – especially the expanses not yet spoilt through the development of tourist accommodation – is revealed to the walker alone. The same can be said for the primary-rock mountain chains of the Serra de Monchique and the Serra do Caldeirão. Here one feels light years away from the hustle and bustle of the coast. For those seeking absolute peace and quiet, the west coast, exposed to the Atlantic, with its vast landscapes of dunes and wild foaming seas will hopefully rest long as a Sleeping Beauty until Prince Tourist-trade Tycoon awakes her with a capitalistic kiss. The Sotavento (»protected from the wind«) region of the eastern Algarve also promises quiet, peaceful walking. Here walkers drawn to an unspoilt natural environment will enjoy a heavenly spectrum starting with secluded islands, progressing to a verdant and flowering hinterland and culminating in the barren mountain region on the border of Alentejo.

The 51 walks contained in this guide cannot possibly include all of the worth-while routes of the Algarve. They are selected primarily to inspire the walker to discover unknown stretches of coast and hinterland for himself – along these walks and along new ones.

Flora

Just as the geological composition of the individual regions of the Algarve are quite different, just so diverse is the flora we enjoy in our walks. On the sandy soil over which our coastal paths lead, grow not only different varieties of grass (although in summer mostly withered) – but also a multitude of wildflowers. Grass provides protection for many species of orchids and narcissus, including the tiny jonquil. Where the earth is more alkaline, varieties of colourful orchids cluster together in close quarters with the endemic dwarf palm. Right up to the edges of the coastal cliffs, we can enjoy the yellow flowers of the spotted rock rose, Algarve daisies, iris, hyacinth, flowering kale and – blooming into the summer months – other cistus bushes which, along with other varieties of flowering shrubs, make up the *phrygana*. Year-round, this knee-high scrubby undergrowth delights the walker with lovely scents of essential oil, released when brushed up against, more than it hinders his stride. In the far west, we encounter only scant ground cover, however the more east we go, the denser the scrub and brush becomes. A *macchia* vegetation which can grow to a height of 2 m and more when intertwined with trees creates such a thicket that the walker faces what appears to be an impassable obstacle. The Portuguese term *matos* denotes the entire spectrum of scrub vegetation included in *macchia* and *phrygana*.

The summit view at Rocha dos Soidos.

Trees characterise almost every natural landscape through which we walk in the Algarve. In a country that produces 50 % of the world's cork, we can expect to encounter the cork oak time and again. The first cork harvest takes place as soon as the tree, with its many branches, reaches the age of 30. Every 9 years thereafter, an additional bark-peeling is undertaken and the harvest year is painted on the trunk to keep track of the last »shearing«. Quietude flows naturally from a long cycle such as this and since each individual »cork factory« needs a lot of space to grow, a cork oak forest takes on the semblance of a park. The closer we come to the *Serras*, the more frequently we will encounter this so typically Portuguese tree.

Almond trees, blooming in springtime with flowers in colours ranging from white to violet which produce the sweet nuts in the autumn, can be encountered everywhere in the hilly countryside of the Barlavento. In the fertile alkaline shed of the Barrocal, the almond is joined by evergreen trees of olive and carob.

The further we forge ahead toward the east, the more we encounter citrus groves, often emitting a pleasant perfume, as well as quince and fig trees bearing fruit which, when combined with almonds, provide the basis for many a delicious sweet. The *matos* vegetation, typical for this region, is a combination of the thorny Holm oak, bushy olive scrub and wild jasmine along with the white-flowering rock rose (cistus). The walker would do well to avoid the thorns and spikes of this trail companion, flowering colourfully in springtime. The eucalyptus tree is an interloper to the region but has increased rapidly in numbers – thanks also to the support of the EU. Already this tree makes up 60 % of the reforested areas since the paper industry needs cellulose and the eucalyptus grows quickly. Some people are concerned about the effects of this monoculture on the environment since the trees need a lot of water and deplete the ground water to the detriment of other trees and plants. Moreover, fallen eucalyptus leaves cover the ground in such a way that most of the underbrush is unable to grow. In addition to the cork oak, the acidic soil found in the slate rock of the *Serras* north of the

Solitude on a bay near Benagil.

Markets

Markets are regularly held in almost every large settlement in the Algarve. Here is a summary of the most original:

Albufeira: 1st and 3rd Tuesday in the month; Alcoutim: May 1, Potter's Market with folk dancing; Estói: every 2nd Sunday in the month; Faro: 1st Friday und Saturday in the month (flowers!); Lagos: every Saturday at the bus station; Loulé: every Saturday around the market hall; Moncarapacho: every 1st Sunday in the month; Monchique: October 26-28 (a broad range of merchandise!); Olhao: every Saturday; Pereiro: every 4th Sunday in the month; Quarteira: every Wednesday; São Brás de Alportel: every Saturday.

Sport

In addition to walking, the Algarve offers ideal conditions for mountain-biking – especially in the countryside and in the Monchique hills. Some of the described walks can be also undertaken by mountain bike. Numerous golf courses, very creatively laid out, offer greens that are recognized as some of Europe's most beautiful.

The Atlantic Coast allows for all types of water sport, from wind surfing to sailing to board surfing (preferred areas include the west and south-west coasts all the way to Praia Zavial) as well as water-skiing and diving. Especially on the cliffs of the west coast and between Lagos and the Cap São Vicente attractive diving areas await you.

Excursions by boat

In many cities along the southern coast, excursions by boat are offered along the coastline. These can also be incorporated into some of the coastal walks. Highly recommended is the boat trip from Lagos to Ponta de Piedade. Also especially attractive are the riverboat tours on the Rio Arade from Portimão to Silves and from Vila Real along the Rio Guadiana.

Beaches

»Whosoever cannot find a favourite beach in the Algarve is certainly beyond help.« Few regions are able to offer such a variety of selections for the ocean-loving tourist – from the cliff-girdled dangerously wave-battered beaches of the west coast, where swimming should be restricted to beaches where life guards hold watch, through to the small inlets and grand sandy bays of the cliff-coast Algarve and the nearly endless sand shores of the islands of the Sotavento and finally the river and stream banks of the hinterland.

The Algarve must certainly accommodate every visitor with his personal favourite beach – he only has to look for it. The described walks lead to many of most beautiful beaches in the Algarve.

Festivals

End of January/beginning of February: Almond Blossom Festival in Vilamoura; February: Mardi Gras / Shrove Tuesday (esp. in Loulé, Moncarapacho, Portimão); February/March: Grain Festival in Salir, Sausage Festival in Alte, 2nd Sunday after Easter: Festa da Mae Soberana in Loulé; May 1: Festa da Grande Fonte in Alte; June 13: Festival of Saint Anthony in Faro; June: Festival de Cerveja – beer festival in Silves; Middle July: Feira do Carmo – grand local fair in Faro; July 17: Procession on the Sea in Fuzeta – Festa do Carmo; August: Sardine Festival in Olhao; September: Festa do Beato Sao Vicente in Albufeira; October: Feira de Santa Iria – grand annual fair in Faro, October: October Market in Monchique.

Barrocal supports, fairly monotone vegetation with tree heather, lavender and common heather. Only the flowers of the shiny-leaf rock rose stand out. In contrast, a larger variety of flora can be found in the Monchique hills due to the higher elevations and granite rock. Here we can also encounter the strawberry tree, in September and October flowering in snow-white while bearing red fruit at the same time. The best way to enjoy this fruit is in its liquid form – served up as *Medronho* schnapps.

Fauna

While most visitors in the Algarve are primarily interested in the creatures of the sea – and rightly so, since here the best selection of fresh seafood in all of Europe appears on the dinner table – the country folk are not left completely empty-handed. Here we can find a vast spectrum of our feathered friends, from the flamingos in the Ria Formosa Natural Park to the songbirds in the river deltas of the countryside and in the Monchique hills.

The beasts of the earth are more difficult to find. Hunting fever is not the least of the threats to the scanty populations of rabbits, wild pigs and everything in between. Little-loved critters such as snakes, scorpions and insects have been already covered under the topic »Dangers«. Fortunately, the rustle in the undergrowth is usually caused by harmless lizards and geckos.

Natural Parks and Nature Reserves

Our walking tours in the Algarve encompass both of the major natural parks as well as a number of smaller nature reserves. The »Parque Natural de

Country companion – a friendly wandering goat.

Sudoueste Alentejano e Costa Vicentina« (Walks 23 and 24) includes the entire west coast of Alentejo and the Algarve to the south up to Praia do Burgau (Walks 1–5). Connecting to the east, starting at the Ilha do Faro and stretching even further beyond Tavira is an additional expanse of protected coastline »Parque Natural da Ria Formosa« (Walks 18–22) followed by the »Reserva Natural do Sapal de Castro Marim e Vila Real de Santo António« at the bordering river Rio Guadiana (Walk 49).

Smaller nature reserves contain the »Rocha da Pena« (Walk 38) near Alte, parts of the Serra de Monchique (Walk 28–31), the lagoons on the Ria de Alvor (Walk 8), the banks of the Rio Arade north of Portimao (Walk 32), the dunes near Monte Gordo (Walk 22), the »Fonte Benémola« near Querenca north of Loulé (Walk 42) and also the Mata Nacionales near Barão de S. João (Walk 25), near Tavira (Walk 48) and near Odeleite (Walks 50 and 51). While the coastal parks have been established mainly to protect the many species of wild birds found there, both of the small inland parks focus on exceptional geological and historical features presented in detail in the individual walk descriptions for those regions.

Geology

Portugal is bordered on three sides by the ocean – this fact alone promises spectacular walks along dramatic coastlines. The narrow strip of sand of the Litorial along the southern coast was created by the erosion of the limestone surface. The properties of this fertile soil allow little protection from evaporation so in summer it turns dry and brown.

The alkaline countryside of the Barrocal foothills follows, with fantastic and picturesque crags, especially in the Barlavento. In-between lie fertile valleys of heavy acidic loam »terra rossa« (red earth) where the bounty of the land flourishes but also provides a haven for areas of impassable *macchia*.

In the north, the lofty granite-based mountain regions of the »Serras«, stretching to the east as far as the bordering Guadiana River, are particularly alluring due to their great solitude. The highest peaks – offering lovely views – can be found on the Fóia and the Picota in the Serra de Monchique.

To the west, no less secluded, lie the towering black slate cliffs of the dramatic coast.

Picnic Places

The Portuguese love to picnic in pretty surroundings in the great outdoors. In many places where the natural landscape is lovely, beautiful picnic areas have been constructed, often near a source of water. Some of these have been incorporated into several of the described walks, e.g. Mata Nacional de Barão de S. João (Walk 25), Fonte near Paderne (Walk 34), Fontes in Alte (Walks 36 and 37), Fonte Benemola (Walk 42) and Fonte Ferrea (Walk 43).

Information and Addresses

Getting there

The international airport for the Algarve is Faro. Many chartered and scheduled airlines like TAP (Air Portugal) and Portugália provide service to here.

Information

Great Britain: ICEP – Portuguese Trade and Tourism Office, 2nd Floor, 22–25a Sackville Street, London, W1S 3LY. Tel. Brochure Line: 0906 364 0610 (calls cost 60p per minute at all times) Tel. Enquiries: 020 7494 5720, Fax: 020 7494 1868

Portuguese Embassy, 11, Belgrave Square, London, SW1X 8PP, Tel Brochure Line: 0845 355 1212, Fax: 020 7201 6633, www.portugalinsite.com

U.S.A.: Portuguese National Tourist Office, 590 Fifth Ave, New York, NY 10036, Tel. 212 354 4403, www.portugal.org.

Portugal: Direcçao-General do Tourismo, Av. António Augusto Aguiar 86, 1069-021 Lisbon. Tel. 00351 21 3575086, Fax: 3575220, www. dgtourismo.pt. Faro: Rua da Misericórdia 8–12, Tel.00351 89 80360, Airport Tel. 00351 89 818582. Região de Tourismo do Algarve, Rta. Av. 5 de Outobro, 8002 Faro. Tel. 00351 289 800400, Fax: 00351 289 800489.

Artistic chimneys ...

... competing with flowers.

Tourist offices can be found in all of the major and some of the smaller cities in the Algarve, providing information concerning the immediate area and its environs as well as for public transport. These offices can also be quite helpful in the search for accommodation.

Climate

In the Algarve, the walker can expect the typical Mediterranean climate with hot summers that are eased by the cool winds off the Atlantic. Springtime usually begins already in February. Starting in October, scattered rainfall can be expected triggering a »second spring« greening. Water temperatures are somewhat lower on the west coast when matched against those in the southern Algarve (in midsummer 18 deg. compared to 19–22 deg. C).

CLIMATE TABLE FOR ALGARVE												
Month	1	2	3	4	5	6	7	8	9	10	11	12
Air (max./ °C)	15	16	18	20	22	25	28	28	26	22	19	16
Air (min./°C)	9	10	11	13	14	18	20	20	19	16	13	10
Water (°C)	16	15	16	16	17	18	19	20	20	19	17	16
Rainy days	9	7	10	6	4	1	0	0	2	6	8	9

Camping

Along the Algarve Coasts, numerous campgrounds can be found (e.g. in Albufeira, Aljezur, Armação de Pêra, Ferragudo, Ingrina, Lagos, Monte Gordo, Olhão, Portimão, Quarteira, Sagres, Salema, Tavira, Vila Do Bispo and Vila Real de Santo António); these are graded in quality from one star through four stars. The central tourist office in Lisbon (see »Information«) offers an up-to-date campground guide in multiple languages.

Theft

As in all tourist regions, you can reckon with pickpockets as well as beach and hotel thieves, especially in the coastal centres. As a basic rule, you should never leave anything, and certainly not valuables, in your vehicle – not even in the boot. Vehicle break-ins are common while car theft is rare.

Holidays

January 1: New Year; March/April: Good Friday and Easter Sunday; April 25: Dia da Liberdade – national holiday to commemorate the Carnation Revolution 1974; May 1: Labour Day; May/June: Corpus Christi; June 10: Dia de Portugal; August 15: Mary's Ascension Day; October 5: Dia da Republica – honours the proclamation of the Republic in 1910; November 1: All Saint's Day; December 1: Dia da Restauração – commemorates the end of Spanish foreign rule 1640; December 8: Immaculate Conception of the Virgin Mary; December 25: Christmas Day.

Emergency phone numbers
The collective number for emergency medical assistance, ambulance and the fire department: Tel. 115 (free of charge).
Police emergency: Tel. 112.
Apothecary emergency service: Tel. 118.
Breakdown service: Tel. 01 9425095 (Portuguese Automobile Club).

Telephone
The dialling code from Portugal to Great Britain is 0044. The dialling code to Portugal is 00351.

Accommodation
A wide selection of accommodation of all categories, especially along the southern coast of the Algarve, is available. In the preface to the individual walks, overnight quarters away from tourist centres are indicated. Many walkers may be interested in accommodation offered through »Turismo de Habitação« and »Turismo Rural«. Information: ENATUR, Av. Santa Joana Princesa 10, 1749 Lisbon. Tel. 218 442039. Fax: 218 442088.

Public transport
The public transport system served by bus is very good in the coastal regions.
From Lagos to Vila Real, a railway line runs parallel to the coastline (in the west sometimes kilometres inland) offering an inexpensive means of travel although the going is slow due to numerous stops. The latest timetables can be picked up at any railway station. Car hire is offered at reasonable prices at the airport in Faro, in all the major tourist centres and in most hotels.
Taxis are available in all the cities and larger settlements. Especially when more people are involved, taxis offer a flexible, relatively inexpensive alternative to public transport and to car hire.
For excursions into the countryside, a private vehicle is an absolute must. The roads are sometimes narrow but mostly surfaced. Until the motorway running parallel is finally completed, the EN 125 west of Faro will continue to be a bottleneck prone to traffic jams. Along this stretch and along the winding inland country roads, expect confrontation with Portuguese speed merchants as well as with motor cars that are poorly lit at night – sometimes without any lamps at all!

Bus stations are found in the following larger settlements:
Albufeira: Av. da Liberdade, Tel. 289 513650
Armação de Pêra: Av. da Liberdade, Tel. 282 312494
Faro: Av. da Republica: Tel. 289 899-760 -761 -709
Lagos: Rossio S. Joao, Tel. 282 762944

Monte Gordo – Agente – Tel. 281 541466
Olhão: Av. General H. Delgado, Tel. 289 702157
Portimão: Largo do Dique, Tel. 282 23211
Quarteira: Av. Project. Ap. Golfo Mar, Tel. 289 389143
Tavira: Praça da Repubblica, Tel. 281 322546
Vilamoura: Aldeia do Mar, Tel. 289 302635
Vila Real de S. António: Av. da Republica, Tel. 281 511807

As a rule, bus service at the weekend is reduced considerably from that offered on weekdays. Detailed information is available through the bus stations listed above, through the local and regional tourist offices or on the internet under www.eva-transportes.pt. Bus schedules are also often posted on kiosks.

You can only get there on foot – beach near Albufeira.

The Barlavento Coastlines (Western Algarve)

Spectacular coastlines with sandstone cliff formations, splendid beaches of red and white sands, the pristine waters of the Atlantic and, last but not least, a seemingly endless selection of accommodation and leisure activities – these are the things that attract most tourists to spend their holidays in the Algarve. In the Barlavento, the stretch of the south coast exposed to the wind between Sagres and Faro, you can be assured that every expectation called forth by Algarve brochures achieves fulfilment.

Just how diverse the western portion of the Algarve coast really is, should be well-illustrated in the 18 coastal walks described in this section. These are designed to inspire the walker to discover lesser-known but not less-exciting coastal regions. The walks lead along spectacular cliff formations to delightful beaches, pass through picturesque coastal villages and through a surprising variety of different landscapes and vegetation.

Long-distance walk enthusiasts can easily combine the various linear and circular routes to create a personal walking itinerary, choosing from the 8 to 10 stretches between Sagres and Faro that encompass the entire spectrum of the Barlavento coastlines.

For a staged walk, over-night accommodation as well as restaurants and bars are available in Sagres, Salema or Burgau, Luz, Lagos, Portimão, Carvoeiro or Benagil, Armação de Pêra, Albufeira, Quarteira and finally in Faro.

Mass tourism in Armação de Pêra ...

… and the massive cliffs of Ponta da Piedade.

1 From Sagres to Praia do Zavial

A walk along the south-westernmost edge of Europe

Sagres – Ponta dos Caminhos – Praia da Ingrina – Praia do Zavial

Starting point: Sagres, 20 m. Hourly bus service to Lagos. By car: Via the N 268, from the central square Praça da Republica along the Rua Comandante Metoso to Porto da Baleeira. Parking possible (a bus stop is also located on this spot).

Destination: Praia do Zavial, 0 m. Bus station for the Sagres – Lagos line in Raposeira, 4 km away on the EN 125.

Walking times: Sagres – Ponta dos Caminhos ¾ hr, Ponta dos Caminhos – Praia da Ingrina 1¾ hr, Praia da Ingrina – Praia do Zavial ½ hr; total time 3 hr (9.2 km).

Ascent: 230 m of ascents and descents.

Grade: Due to the many forks in the paths along the route, orientation problems make this walk a little more difficult.

Refreshments: Restaurants in Sagres,
beach bars in Martinhal, Praia da Ingrina and Zavial as well as in Raposeira (see Alternatives).

Alternatives: 1. Especially after periods of rainfall, it is recommended to begin this walk in Poco (bus stop) north of Sagres. From there, a good 1 km to Praia do Martinhal.

2. Ending the walk on the Praia do Barranco João Vaz or on the Praia da Ingrina: from either bay, dusty roads lead to the hamlet of Raposeira (bus stop) 4 km away on the E 125.

3. After not quite an hour from Zavial, along a narrow, little-used tarmac road via Hortas do Tabual to Raposeira (bus line Sagres – Lagos).

Tip: Visits to the Fortaleza de Sagres and the Cabo de São Vicente are absolute »musts« for this tour.

A barren, solitary landscape, whipped by wild winds, with panoramic views and secluded beaches – this walk covers the western-most part of the Algarve's south coast.

Many cliffs to cross.

Begin the walk at the fishermen's harbour in **Sagres** and with our backs to the ocean, ascend along the steps. In front of the restaurant »Tascas«, continue the ascent again over steps to the right and along a path to **Praia da Baleeira**, where picturesque fishing boats are beached. On the other side of a cliff, reach the wind-blown Praia do Martinhal after 1.5 km. Cross to the other end of the beach then ascend along distinct paths to the top of the coastal cliffs. Skirt around the steep cliff **Ponta dos Caminhos** after another 1.5 km by walking somewhat inland. Now return to the cliff's brink and follow the path running parallel and high above the foaming sea.

After 3.5 km, descend along paths to the next beach below: **Praia do Barranco João Vaz**. 600 m further on, again along a steeply ascending trail starting at the end of the narrow beach, continue straight on for another 300 m along a path until reaching a fork; bear left here. Passing through thickets of matos vegetation, continue walking for another 1.5 km until reaching a descending dusty road that drops down to the right and to **Praia da Ingrina**.

Now our route ahead veers somewhat away from the coastline. Directly on the other side of the car park, turn right and away from the tarmac road and use paths to cross over a small hill. Now cross over a dirt track to continue the ascent following a line of concrete posts to the next hill. Here descend to a country lane and along this, now 500 m away from the car park, turn right towards the ocean for another 50 m. Turn left onto a path that ascends and returns to the panoramic coastline above some sheer cliffs.

Cross over another trail and descend through the thick brush undergrowth bearing left towards the beach bar. Here the flat bay at **Zavial** begins, perfect for a long break and a swim.

2   To Praia do Zavial and Praia das Furnas

Circular walk in the Algarve's »Wild West«

Figueira – Hortas do Tabual – Ingrina – Praia do Zavial – Praia das Furnas – Figueira

Starting point and destination: Figueira, 50 m. Bus stop for the Lagos – Sagres line. By car: The turn-off from the N 125 is signposted for »Salema«. In Figueira, parking is possible in the village centre along the road to Praia da Figuera.

Walking times: Figueira – Hortas do Tabual ¾ hr, Hortas do Tabual – Praia da Ingrina ¾ hr, Praia da Ingrina – Praia do Zavial ½ hr, Praia do Zavial – Praia das Furnas ¾ hr, Praia das Furnas – Figueira ¾ hr; total time 3½ hr (13.7 km).

Ascent: 180 m of ascents and descents.

Grade: Mostly easy, although strenuous along the steep ascent at the other end of Praia do Zavial

Refreshments: Beach bars on all of the beaches along the route.

Tip: The Guadelupe church situated on the EN 125 – one of the few not destroyed by an earthquake in 1755 – is well worth a visit.

Even scant vegetation and austere scenery can have a certain charm. This is well-illustrated on our walk, crossing through the arid terra firma of the western Algarve. A number of beautiful and still secluded beaches offer good long breaks for swimming.

From the bus stop or from the parking places in the centre of the sleepy village of **Figueira**, walk along the village street towards Sagres (west) and after 400 m, at the village limits, cross over a bridge. Directly after, turn left

The descent to Praia das Furnas.

onto a country lane. On the rise in front of us to our right, we can enjoy the view of an old windmill. Upon reaching a trail turning off to the left, continue straight on for 600 m before reaching a trail junction which we cross straight over. After a 400 m stretch of descent, reach yet another trail crossing (sign to the left »Praia«). At this point, Walk 3 forks left to Praia das Furnas. Our return route also merges here. Now, however, we continue in the same direction as before.

Cross over a stream bed then pass a farmhouse on our left and after another 400 m ascent, cross over yet another intersecting trail. Climbing downward, the hamlet **Hortas do Tabual** appears before us. Before we can reach it, however, we must skirt around a hill by bearing right. 1.3 as well as 1.5 km after the last trail crossing, ignore the trails forking off to the right. Cross over a stream bed then head left to the houses of the village.

Here, ignore the first side street. Only upon reaching the centre do we turn right onto the main street. Forthwith, in front of the church at a water trough, turn left along a side street which after a few metres joins the road connecting Raposeira and Zavial. Cross this road and continue on in the same direction as before.

Pass over a little valley with trees, ignore a fork to the right and follow the rocky trail that swings left. 750 m after leaving the village behind, we pass a house on our left. Swing right along a track then bear right when the track bends to the left. Ascend along the row of telegraph poles and 1 km after passing the house reach the hamlet of **Ingrina**.

Meeting up with a small tarmac street, follow this to the right for a few metres then immediately turn diagonally to the left onto a street (signposted »Ingrina Campsite«). Since it is not permitted to cross through this area, after reaching the entrance 400 m on, turn right along a narrow path to skirt around the campground and a eucalyptus grove, both lying to our left. Then turn right onto a trail ascending from the campground then ignore the trail forking off to the left and continue in a long swing to the left remaining on the widest dirt road and descending to **Praia da Ingrina**. Meet up with a tarmac road, follow this shortly left and then bear right to reach the bay and the beach bar.

At the eastern side of the beach bar, cross over the car park then immediately turn right and away from the tarmac road. An ascent follows then descend to the left to a dirt road where a path ascends along a row of concrete posts. 500 m beyond the car park meet up with a track and follow this right only to swing immediately left onto a cliff path. Passing through thick underbrush, descend steeply to the left to reach a café and Zavial's Beach.

Along the cliffs, follow the beach for a while leading somewhat away from the coastline until reaching the eastern end and the next steep ascent that opens up a fantastic backwards view of the sandy bay. The ascent continues to the left, then right until we meet an intersecting trail 1 km past the Bay of Zavial. Follow this to the right to **Ponta da Torre**.

Unfortunately, all that remains of the former watchtower is a large pile of stones. Here enjoy a panoramic view reaching from Sagres to the far west all the way to Lagos to the east.

Having descended 300 m along a footpath to the left, a trail merges from the left. Continue straight on this trail keeping parallel to the coast for 1 km. As soon as the trail bears left and away from the coastline, turn right onto a path. Again at the fork immediately following, bear right and after descending for another 300 m meet up with an intersecting trail in a little valley. Turn left here and continue on through the undergrowth. During the descent ignore the first footpaths forking right and in a sweep to the right keep heading towards the far end of the **Praia das Furnas**. The descent to the beach is made in steep and numerous zigzags.

It is reassuring to know that nothing stands in the way of another break for bathing in this lovely bay since the return route is simple. Follow the dirt road up the valley, fording the stream bed time and again. After 250 m bear right and after another 250 m bear diagonally left. The merge that we reach after a good 1.5 km is easy to recognize. On the approach route, here by the signpost »Praia«, we had continued straight on. So now turn right and in hilly ascents and descents finally reach the tarmac road turning right and return to the village centre of **Figueira**.

It is worth continuing for another 2 km to visit the charming church Nossa Senhora de Guadalupe either on foot or by car along the N 125 west. The church is on the right-hand side of the road and displays Romanesque and Gothic adornments. Legend has it that Prince Henry the Navigator gave thanks here when an adventurous voyage came to a happy end. Hopefully, you can do the same yourself and for the same reason!

Our destination, the Praia das Furnas.

3   To Praia das Furnas and Praia da Figueira

Along spirited coastal paths to secluded beaches

Figueira – Praia das Furnas – Praia da Figueira – Salema – Figueira

Starting point and destination: Figueira, 50 m. Bus stop for the Lagos – Sagres line. By car: take the N 125 from Lagos, 1 km past Budens turn left (sign »Salema«) then immediately turn right. Car park in the village centre.
Walking times: Figueira – Praia das Furnas ¾ hr, Praia das Furnas – Praia da Figueira 1 hr, Praia da Figueira – Salema ¾ hr, Salema – Figueira ½ hr; total time 3 hr (12.4 km).

Ascent: 370 m of ascents and descents.
Grade: Strenuous walk along trails and cliff footpaths with steep, sometimes slippery ascents and descents.
Refreshments: In Figueira and in Salema. In Salema hotels and private accommodation are also available.
Alternative: Starting from the Praia da Figueira you can return in ½ hr to Figueira along a track and thereby shorten the walking tour.

This is a route for walkers who love nature in its pristine form. Follow Walk 2 until reaching the signpost »Praia«. Turn left and after another 1.2 km descend to a stream bed. Turn left again to reach the delightful **Praia das Furnas** after about 300 m.
Head left towards the east end of the beach and continue for 20 m towards a towering crag. Behind the crag, ascend along the traces of a path. After a 500 m long ascent reach the end of the climb. Continue left ascending again towards an odd, architecturally utopian house. In front of this, turn right onto a path that soon becomes a trail. 200 m on, in a left bend, continue straight ahead along a path that reaches a trail in a natural depression after 100 m. Turn right on the trail and follow it to the edge of the cliff. At the

Sweeping view from the Praia das Furnas to Ponta de Sagres.

end of the trail, turn left along a path along the rim above the coastline. 500 m on, reach the highest point at a wall. Turn right along the wall then continue towards another natural depression. Now continue straight on the path and reach another rise in a 500 m long climb and another rise again 500 m further on. Now the path steeply descends until it almost reaches a small sandy bay. Climb up the slope on the other side of the bay and after 600 m meet up with a trail. Bear right here in a final steady descent and along the broadest trail. After 1.2 km through a slippery scree-covered slope reach the **Praia da Figueira**.

The next leg now leads with less difficulty along a stream heading up the valley for 50 m and then crosses the stream over stepping stones. Continue for 300 m in a right-to-left zigzag ascent to reach the medieval **Fort of Figueira**. Now walk mainly on the level parallel to the coastline and after 300 m turn left ascending along the rim of a valley. After another 700 m bear right descending to the valley floor. Along a broader track continue right, ascending to the next rise. At a fork, bear right to reach the first houses of **Salema** 500 m on. Keeping to the right of the villas, on the side nearest the sea, descend along the broadest path, keeping parallel to the coastline and enjoy lovely views until finally reaching **Praia da Salema**.

To return to Figueira, begin at the square at the back of the beach and walk along the stream. Cross over after 50 m and start a steep ascent left along an old cobblestone lane. A dusty road then leads after 2 km past the house »Monte Palmares«. To our left, a high hill sports an antennae installation and **Figueira** has already appeared before us. In the village, turn left onto the main street – passing the intersection of the signposted road ascending from Praia Figueira – to return to the car park.

4　To the Monolith of Aspradantes

A ramble with diversity but lacking in shade

Praia das Furnas – Monolith of Aspradantes – Praia das Furnas

Starting point and destination: Praia das Furnas, 0 m. Bus service only to Figueira. By car: follow the directions to Figueira (see Walk 3). At the western village limits and directly after the bridge, bear left then immediately right; after 1.2 km (signposted »Praia«) and after another 1.3 km again to the left. Parking possible at the end of the dusty road as far as you can drive.

Walking times: Praia das Furnas – Monolith ¾ hr, Monolith – Praia das Furnas ½ hr; total time 1¼ hr (4.3 km).

Ascent: 80 m of ascents and descents.

Grade: This is an easy ramble along dusty roads and paths that are sometimes rocky.

Refreshments: Nothing available at the beach or along the route.

Alternative: Easy to combine with Walks 2 or 3 – also for the approach and return from or to Figueira.

A short walk, embracing all the lovely elements of the western Algarve into a nice package; a delightful and secluded sandy beach nestled in a cliff-encircled bay, a stream to cross again and again, a zealously farmed countryside behind the first coastal foothills – lushly greening and flowering in the springtime – and to top it all off, one of the oldest monuments in the Algarve, perched upon a panoramic hillock.

From the car park, at first cross a stream bed heading down the valley for the last 150 m until reaching **Praia the Furnas**, a splendid sandy beach picturesquely surrounded by steep cliffs. After a refreshing dip in the sea, begin the walk to the ancient monolith.

Head back 400 m up the valley crossing over the stream and passing the car park until reaching the fork in the trail. We have already been at this point arriving from the right but now we bear left, ascending gently along a country lane until reaching a panoramic rise. Bear right at a fork 600 m further onto a trail (the trail to the left leads to Praia do Zavial). After 200 m bear right onto a narrower trail and after another 100 m bear left through an abandoned sheepfold. Our destination is the summit of the hillock to our right. As we come nearer, we can make out a light-coloured block

34

of rock and a beaten footpath leading to it another 150 m further on. The ascent is not only worth while due to the more than 4000 year-old **Monolith of Aspradantes** (supposedly in the same position in the middle of a stone circle where it was originally erected) but also because a fantastic 360° view presents the entire southwest coast and its hilly hinterland spread out below us.

After enjoying our fill of this sight, retrace along the ascending path for 150 m. Now turn left onto a trail passing through open *matos* vegetation then 300 m on descend right to the edge of a field. Follow along the field on the right-hand side then descend right to the walls of a house; continue past these to our left. Now the route follows a path to reach the country lane already used on our approach route. A left turn leads in a few minutes to the fork then after a right turn, only 400 m lie between us and another exhilarating plunge in the sea.

4000 years old: the monolith of Aspradantes.

5 From Burgau to Salema

To a Roman villa and to gorgeous, inviting beaches on the former rice belt

Burgau – Praia de Almádena – Boca do Rio – Salema

Starting point: Burgau, 10 m. End of the bus line from Lagos via Luz. By car: from the N 125 9.5 km west of Lagos, turn left. Parking possible on the side of the broad street to the right behind the bus station.

Destination: Salema, 10 m. Bus service to Sagres and Lagos. From the N 125: 1 km past Budens turn left.

Walking times: Burgau – Praia de Almádena ¾ hr, Praia de Almádena – Boca do Rio ½ hr, Boca do Rio – Salema ½ hr; total time (6.3 km).

Ascent: 270 m of ascents and descents.

Grade: Some steep ascents and descents make this uncomplicated walk more difficult.

Refreshments: Bars and restaurants in Burgau and Salema; at the time of writing, no refreshments available en route.

Alternatives: 1. Walkers choosing to return to Burgau (no direct bus connections!), aside from using the coastal route, can take the access road on the other side of the Boca do Rio 250 m to reach the tarmac connecting road and continue the return to Burgau along this (1½ hr).

2. The tarmac road which runs parallel along the same route Salema – Burgau – Luz almost the entire way and lies between 200 and 1000 m away while following the groundwork of the old trail connecting the villages, presents the possibility of finishing the tour at any time on a paved surface.

Important notice: A construction area may block both the descent to and the ascent from Burgau. You should skirt around to the east to avoid this site.

This is an attractive walk along a rugged coastline encompassing a number of ascents and descents but also offering phenomenal pristine natural landscapes and brilliant bathing beaches. This is the author's favourite coastal walk in the Barlavento.

»The Romans' bay« Boca do Rio.

Begin at the bus stop in **Burgau** and walk west along the street. After 200 m, at the village limits, turn left onto a path that ascends steeply for 250 m to a cliff high above the coast. At the end, the path drops down to the right through a natural depression. After a short ascent to win back our height, pass through a second small valley just before making a 500 m long, steep ascent to finally reach the peninsula **Ponta de Almádena**.

At the start of the descent after 1.5 km, meet up with an intersecting trail and follow this for 200 m left to reach the overlook at the tip of the peninsula. Then retrace the route for 250 m to turn left onto the path leading to **Praia de Almádena**. Continue right until reaching a tumbledown building and then turn left to descend to the beach.

At the other end of the beach, climb up along a path or over steps to the next cliff. After 350 m and in front of a house, descend to the right to a small road. Immediately turn left and return to the coastal footpath heading towards the medieval fort. Cross over to the left, then bear to the right of the ruins and descend steeply to the right to the **bay at Boca do Rio**. For the final few metres, follow a track to the left and cross over the **Ribeira de Vale Barão** on stepping stones. When walking this trail in the opposite direction, it is important to turn right 50 m after crossing the stream and behind the tumbledown building onto a somewhat indistinct ascending path.

At the opposite end of the sprawling bay, a fenced-in area stretching to the waterline encompasses the ruins of buildings from the Roman era. We rush on continuing along paths to ascend the next cliff and after 150 m meet up with a dusty road and then keep parallel to the coastline. When this swings right 500 m on, continue straight ahead for another 300 m along the coast until reaching a house that blocks a direct route to Salema. Turn right here and after a 250 m descent, meet up with a tarmac road; turn left here. Following this road, our walk becomes a promenade for the last 700 m via the Rua dos Pescadores passing through the oldest, very well-preserved part of the village and ending at the **Praia da Salema**.

6   From Luz to Burgau

Coastal walk to a delightful and convivial seaside village

Luz – Burgau – Luz

Starting point and destination: Luz, 15 m. Bus service to Lagos. By car: from the N 125 2.5 km past Lagos, turn left to Luz (4 km). Parking possible next to the church Senhora da Luz or at the beach on the eastern village limits.

Walking times: Luz – Burgau 1½ hr, Burgau – Luz 1½ hr; total time 3 hr (10.4 km).

Ascent: 150 m of ascents and descents.

Grade: This is an easy walk along sometimes rocky paths, trails and a little-used tarmac road.

Refreshments: Restaurants and beach bars in Luz and Burgau.

Alternative: The walk can also end in Burgau, with a bus connection to Lagos via Luz.

You would like to walk along the spectacular coastal cliffs of the Algarve but you would prefer something fairly leisurely? Here is the perfect circular walk to take in a superb stretch of coastline without a lot of effort. A still typically »sleepy« but genial village is the turnaround point – what more do you need for an unforgettable day of walking along the coast?

Begin at the church in **Luz**. (If you parked at the beach, walk west along the seaside promenade with the ocean to your left and, at the end, turn right to reach the little church Senhora da Luz.) Here continue west (the sea is still to your left) along the Rua Calheta until reaching the village limits. 750 m on, when the track turns right towards the new buildings, continue along the path that bears left and leads to the coastline. Although the sandstone cliffs are only 15 m high here, the red cliff formations are nevertheless stunning.

Continue along the path leading somewhat inland and after 250 m pay close attention not to fall through one of the deep holes that are sometimes devilishly camouflaged by fig trees.

While ascending, skirt around a deep bay after 500 m by swinging to the right and away from the coastline at the same time remaining on the ocean side of the villa complex along a way that is sometimes an improved trail. 1 km on, the path ascends along a flat, panoramic rise but then for the last metres climbs along the only truly steep stretch of this walk.

The rise can also be skirted around to the right along a path, but then the sweeping view of the coast from Lagos to Sagres would be missed. If you like, you can walk to the edge of the cliff to observe the awe-inspiring, never-ending battle of the sea

In Burgau's harbour.

against the cliffs – the constantly moving, unyielding waves always eventually conquering the inflexible stone. Be careful when peering over the shaky cliff's edge!

Now **Burgau** has already appeared before us. After another short ascent, a distinct footpath climbs down to the little fort at the village limits. Continue along the village street to the pretty sandy beach at the fishing harbour of the quiet hamlet. What a contrast to the very lively and tourist-oriented Luz! Here is an ideal spot for a long break on the beach and perhaps a dip in the sea.

To begin the return, walk along the beach then follow the village street to the left along our approach route to return to the fort. Here, bear left along a country lane that leads after 250 m to a windmill that can be seen from afar. The windmill is in very good condition and offers an interesting glimpse into its »wheeling heart«.

After another 100 m reach the narrow tarmac road and follow this right. The road leads over the groundwork of the old connecting trail between Burgau and Luz. Ignore all of the forks that follow, also the tarmac road that forks left after 1.2 km and finally, not quite 5 km in total, return to the church in **Luz**'s centre.

7 To Ponta da Piedade

Coastal walk to a labyrinth of grottoes and rock formations

Luz – Porto de Mós – Ponta da Piedade – Lagos

Starting point: Luz, 10 m. Bus service to Lagos. From the N 125: 2.5 km past Lagos, turn left. 4 km on the main road to Luz, signposted »Praia da Luz«. Car park at the beach.

Destination: Lagos, 10 m. Terminus of the railway line from Faro. Central bus station for the western Algarve. By car: Via the N 125. Parking possible at the village limits (near the footbridge) or at the railway station.

Walking times: Luz – Porto de Mós 1¼ hr, Porto de Mós – Ponta da Piedade ½ hr, Ponta da Piedade – Lagos ¾ hr; total time 2½ hr (11.2 km).

Ascent: 300 m of ascents and descents.

Grade: Due to steep ascents and exposed stretches, a more difficult walk along paths and roads.

Refreshments: Luz, Porto de Mós, Ponta da Piedade, Praia do Camilo, Praia Dona Ana, Lagos.

Alternative: An appealing short-cut for the final kilometres is possible using a boat service offered along the ever-changing coastline and shuttling between Ponta da Piedade and Lagos' old town centre.

Tip: The old town centre of Lagos, our destination, makes for a great sight-seeing tour.

Even mundane tourist guides go into rapture when describing »the Algarve's most beautiful rock formations« – the labyrinth of Ponta da Piedade. Other highlights of this walk are some of the loftiest cliffs and particularly dazzling beaches. It's amazing how close to the Algarve's bustling one-time capital city of Lagos one can find a tranquil natural landscape adorned in wild flowers as well as some almost totally secluded bays.

A delightful sandy beach is only one reason why, starting a very long time ago, **Luz** developed into a lively tourist town. Still, we can soon leave the hurly-burly behind us by heading east from the car park along a cobblestone street through a cluster of villas with the ocean to our right. After 250 m, turn right and immediately afterwards turn left. Our first goal, the obelisk atop of the **Atalaia** can be clearly seen. The narrow street becomes an ascending trail that forks after 400 m. Because of the slippery surface, it is better to avoid the most obvious, direct trail; instead climb up a gentler path that heads left towards a tumbledown building. After 250 m, turn right to the obelisk.

Now we are at 109 m over sea level. It is worth while to take a break here and, still panting for breath, quietly savour the majestic view sweeping from the west all the way to the Monchique hills to the north.

Return to the path that 50 m on swings left and keeps along the coastline. A view to the east opens up, reaching way past our next goal – the lighthouse near the Ponta da Piedade. In the abyss below, the surge of the sea can be heard.

Continue the lofty stride above the steep coastline in pleasant up-and-down walking. Ignore a merging trail from the left after 2 km, then be careful when

descending along the slippery soft sandstone surface to finally reach the beach at **Porto de Mós**. Directly behind the modern beach bar at the eastern end of the beach, pick up the path again. Ascend along steps towards a green-roofed Moorish-style villa (hotel »Villa Esmeralda«) and at the top, turn immediately onto the path forking right. More steps climb the final metres to the crest of the cliffs. Villa and apartment complexes are fenced-in to the left but to the right, the sea view opens up against a dramatic background of towering cliffs.

Cross over a gentle valley notch via a narrow path. After the next rise and 500 m on from Porto de Mós descend steeply along cleverly-laid steps. The newly-constructed footpath spans a sheer cliff and is not suited for walkers with a poor head for heights. Especially during periods of rainfall, this stretch, descending just short of another sandy bay, can be most unplea-

Journey's end: the beaches of Lagos.

sant. 100 m on, when a path to the beach descends right, continue left ascending along steps and returning to the heights of the cliffs. Only another 1 km of undulating walking along a coastal path brings us to the climax of our tour: the lighthouse on the **Ponta da Piedade**. But what a trail this is! Time and again we are lured to the cliff's edge high above the ocean, to overlooks with downward views of caves and grottoes.

Already primed for the experience, the variety of rock formations may not surprise us here on the Ponta da Piedade; all the more breathtaking is the view of the coast stretching far over the high-rises of Portimão and beyond. We can also turn right along the dilapidated bridge to enjoy an even more spectacular view from the promontory furthest on. Now descend left along 150 steps to the realm of grottoes and towering sea-stacks. Words cannot describe this scenery – you simply have to walk it yourself!

Return to the heights of the cliffs and cross a car park (in relation to the primary route, turn sharply left). After 150 m, swing right and away from the tarmac road onto a coastal path. 300 m on, cross over a road that leads to one of Lagos' most beautiful beaches – Praia do Camilo. Regrettable, 400 m later we return again to the access road for the lighthouse; turn right here.

If you want to enjoy another fabulous beach, 150 m on, turn right to Praia

Dona Ana; afterwards turn left on a path that leads 500 m to the street at the edge of Lagos' old town. If not, continue along the access road. 500 m further on, cross the main road leading into town. Straight ahead, the access road brings you to the tiny streets and passageways of the picturesque old town replete with restaurants.

It is worth while to take a leisurely sight-seeing ramble. The bus station is located to the north along the coastal road. Reach the railway station by crossing over the footbridge to the other side of the canal.

Filegree: Ponta da Piedade.

8   On the Rio de Alvor

Vast beaches and the Algarve's widest river delta

Lagos – Rio de Alvor – Odiáxere

Starting point: Lagos, 10 m. Terminus of the railway line from Faro. Central bus station for the western Algarve. By car: via the N 125. Parking possible at the village limits (near the footbridge) or at the railway station.
Destination: Odiáxere, 25 m. Train and bus station for the line Lagos – Faro. By car: on the EN 125, 5 km from Lagos.
Walking times: Lagos – mouth of the Rio de Alvor 1½ hr, Rio de Alvor – railway station Odiáxere 1½ hr, railway station Odiáxere – Odiáxere ¾ hr; total time 3¾ hr

(17 km).
Ascent: 120 m of ascents and descents.
Grade: Easy walk along broad trails and sandy beach.
Refreshments: Several beach bars; restaurants in the Palmares Golf Club and in Odiáxere.
Alternative: During the high season, a direct transfer via the mouth of the Rio de Alvor can be made by boat to Alvor.
Tip: In Odiáxere, be sure to visit the village church, sporting a noteworthy manuelin style door.

Again and again, the Algarve surprises us with variances in the natural landscapes that differ considerably from the image presented in brochures. Even as the broad beach Meia Praia at the beginning of our walk becomes more and more deserted, seeming to fulfil a cliché, when we turn away from the seaside, this picture changes abruptly: a vast branching network of tideways and little islands, a paradise for wetland birds (bring along your binoculars!) borders on green gardens and pastureland. Odiáxere, our destination, set away from the EN 125, still preserves the quiet quaintness of a farming village.

We begin our walk at the bus station in **Lagos**, crossing over the broad Avenida dos Descobrimentos and then the Ribeira da Bensafrim over the footbridge by the yacht harbour.

After 300 m we are standing in front of Lagos' railway station. Here turn right following the tracks and, when they swing left, continue straight ahead. Not quite 1 km later, reach the beginning of the longest beach in Lagos, the **Meia Praia**. With the city to our backs (but be sure to turn around to enjoy the view from time to time) we saunter along the beach for 5 km towards the towering hotels of Alvor. To the left, the beach bars beckon, to the right, the ocean, both offer refreshment but of a different kind.

Reaching the moles at the **mouth of the Alvor River**, a decision must be made: take a boat directly to Alvor (see Alternative) or on foot to the village of Odiáxere. The last choice is the nicest. Retrace our beach walk for 1.5 km enjoying the views of this singular lagoon landscape boasting a variety of wetland birds. Cross over the railway tracks to meet up with an ascending dirt road that climbs to the Palmares hill and then turn right onto a tarmac

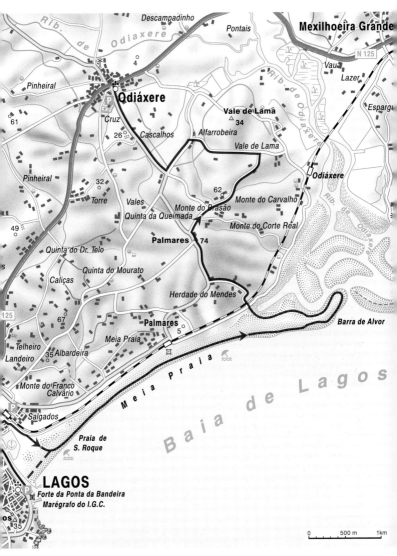

Descampadinho
Pontais
Mexilhoeira Grande
Rib. de Odiaxere
Vau
N 125
Lazer
Pinheiral
4
Espargc
Odiáxere
61
Cruz
Vale de Lamã
△ 34
26
Cascalhos
Alfarrobeira
Vale de Lama
Rib. de Odiáxere
Pinheiral
Odiáxere
32
62
Monte do Carvalho
Torre
Vales
Monte do Brasão
Quinta da Queimada
Monte do Corte Real
49
Palmares 74
Rib. de Odiáxere
Quinta do Dr. Telo
Quinta do Mourato
Caliças
Herdade do Mendes
Barra de Alvor
125
67
Palmares
5
Meia Praia
Telheiro
Albardeira
35
Landeiro
Meia Praia
Monte do Franco
Calvário
Baia de Lagos
Salgados
Praia de
S. Roque
LAGOS
Forte da Ponta da Bandeira
Marégrafo do I.G.C.
os
35

0   500 m   1km

45

road. Continue on this road for 2 km until reaching the boundaries of the Palmares Golf Course.

Past the car park, after enjoying a backwards view of our approach, turn right following the tarmac road and then at the junction 250 m on, turn right again onto a dusty road (signposted »Vale de Lama«). Savour the sweeping view over farmland and river delta while skirting past fields and past a hamlet where it seems time has stood still. After 2 km, the track merges into a tarmac road. Follow the sign-posted road to the left towards **Odiáxere**, 2 km as signposted, and then in front of the village, turn right onto a broad street for the last 2 km.

Lagos: city of shores and sailors.

9   From Alvor to Praia da Rocha

Nature and architects competing as tower-raisers

Alvor – Praia dos Três Irmãos – Praia do Vau – Praia da Rocha

Starting point: Alvor, 20 m. Bus service to Praia da Rocha and Portimão. By car: driving from Faro, 6 km past the Arade bridge, turn left at the signpost for Alvor (5 km). Parking possible at the beach near the high-rise buildings.

Destination: Praia da Rocha, 30 m. Bus service to Alvor and Portimão. Railway station on the northern village limits of Portimão. By car: from Portimão's centre, signposted »Praia da Rocha«.

Walking times: Alvor – Praia dos Três Irmãos ½ hr, Praia dos Três Irmãos – Praia do Vau ¾ hr, Praia do Vau – Praia da Rocha ½ hr; total time 1¾ hr (7.8 km).

Ascent: 130 m of ascents and descents.

Grade: Easy walk along paths and sandy beach.

Refreshments: Numerous beach bars on all the beaches en route.

Alternatives: 1. Along the tarmac road running parallel to the coastal route and often less than 100 m away, busses shuttle back and forth between the starting point and the destination so that the walk can be cut short at anytime. 2. From the coastal trail head, you can choose to turn right instead and walk the 2 km stretch of beach until reaching the moles at the mouth of the Rio de Alvor (see Walk 8).

Tips: Alvor's village centre and the Matriz church there are worth seeing. Boat service is offered along the coast starting at Praia da Rocha.

This is the way the Algarve should be: red-gold towering cliffs, plunging sheer cliff coastlines fronted by tiny inlets and endless beaches, both blessed by spotless white sands. A short walk brings all the expectations of an Algarve holiday-maker to fruition. Of course, this also purports high-rise hotels, born from the flashes of architectural inspiration of the most sundry sort, lining the start of the route and even more so at the end – the

»Algarvehattan« of Praia da Rocha. Begin behind the high-rise buildings over the broad sandy beach of **Praia de Alvor** (with the sea always to the right) towards the cliffs of **Praia dos Três Irmãos**. After 1.5 km, ascend easily to a rise with a superb backwards view over the delta of the Rio de Alvor and all the way to Lagos.

The next hour of walking offers a diverse landscape hard to match. To our right, ever-changing cliff formations and rocky precipices, to our left, snuggled between colourful flowering fields and verdant pine groves, architectural marvels compete in uniqueness. Time and again, descending paths tempt us to little sandy bays huddled between cliffs. Unfortunately, we often have to skirt around properties and sheer drops by cutting inland but always our path returns to the edge of the high coastline.

Towering cliffs and high-rise hotels: Praia da Rocha.

One final deep bay must be crossed but then the skyline of Praia da Rocha appears. After a lovely descent under the scant shade of umbrella pines, reach the edge of **Praia do Vau**. During low tide, we can ramble along the

wide sandy beach between the sea-stacks. At high tide, we must switch to the seaside promenade in front of the high-rise hotels on Praia da Rocha. In the latter case, after not more than 1.5 km, climb the steps back to the beach. Now go through the tunnel »Buraco da Avo« (»hole of the grandmother«) which is cut into the cliffs. At the end of the almost 2 km long beach, ascend along steps to the street. In the Forte de Santa Catarina, one of the restaurants awaits. The bus stop for the line to Portimão and Alvor is nearby.

10 From Ferragudo to Carvoeiro

Shoreline walk, rich in diversity, on the mouth of the Rio Arade

Ferragudo – Ponta do Altar – Praia de Caneiros – Carvoeiro

Starting point: Praia Grande south of Ferragudo, 5 m. Bus service from Portimão to the campground above the Praia Grande. By car: from the N 125 via Portimão and Ferragudo. Parking possible above the beach.

Destination: Carvoeiro, 10 m. Hourly bus service to Lagoa, from there an express bus, Faro – Portimão. By car: from Lagoa via the N 124-1. Parking possible in the village centre.

Walking times: Praia Grande – Ponta do Altar ½ hr, Ponta do Altar – Praia de Caneiros ¼ hr, Praia de Caneiros – Carvoeiro 1½ hr; total time 2¼ hr (8.3 km).

Ascent: 120 m of ascents and descents

Grade: Some steep ascents and descents make this short walk more difficult. Especially during periods of wet weather, sure-footedness and good walking shoes are required.

Refreshments: Beach bars on Praia Grande and Praia de Caneiros, restaurants in Ferragudo and Carvoeiro.

Alternative: Turning back at the Torre de Marinha, return to the starting point along the approach route.

Tip: Ferragudo – with its passageways and seafood restaurants as well as the church there is worth visiting.

This is a coastal walk of another kind. High along the cliffs, passing by beautiful beaches and examples of modern architecture, some marvellous and some missing the mark; at the end, reach the still quaint coastal village of Carvoeiro.

Begin at the **Praia Grande** south of Ferragudo and go left, upriver along the good 500 m long, broad sandy beach. The cliffs on the southern end of the beach are our first goal. Over steps, reach an iron door and then pass

Ferragudo – just like in the Algarve's ancient past.

through a fenced-in property, ascending steeply to the top of the cliff. Here, take the narrow path in the same direction. After 500 m, the trail ends at a car park above the breakwater. To the left of the breakwater, the first beach – the tiny Praia do Pintandinho – offers a break for a swim.

The now broader trail above the cliffs reaches the road 500 m on that leads right and to the lighthouse on the **Ponta do Altar**. Turn left onto a gravel trail that at first heads a little inland and then returns to the cliffs near the beaches. After 500 m, you find yourself standing above the first of the two bays making up the **Praia de Caneiros**. Another 200 m further on and to the right, a footpath descends to the eastern end of the bay. After a break at the beach bar, return to the cliff top and then turn right to pick up one of the trails that either leads near the cliff's edge or further away, mostly level, above the coast and heading west. Our next goal appears: the **Torre de Marinha**, the ruins of a tower built during the Roman era. Reach this ruin high above the sea after another 300 m. At the over 2000 year old remains, you can choose to turn back (see Alternative) and use the approach route to return to Ferragudo. Unfortunately, the route ahead to Carvoeiro passes more and more through hotel and apartment complexes built into the hilly landscape.

Walk another 1 km further, along a broad level trail on the edge of the cliff high above the sea until a path drops down to the **Bay of Mato Serrão**.

On the other end of the bay, continue another 2 km of mostly level walking above the coastline. Now the trail passes between the houses of the picturesque village centre of **Carvoeiro**, to the sandy bay, hemmed in by steep cliff walls.

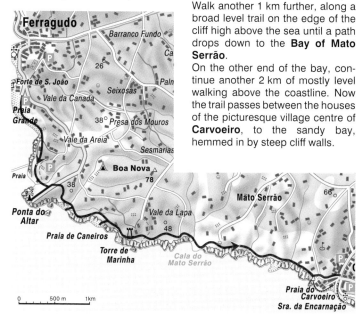

11 The grottoes of Algar Seco near Carvoeiro

Along panoramic cliffs to the prettiest caves in the Algarve

Carvoeiro – Algar Seco – Praia de Vale de Santianes – Carvoeiro

Starting point and destination: Carvoeiro, 50 m. Hourly bus service to the express-bus station in Lagoa on the N 125. By car: from Lagoa via the N 124-1 to Carvoeiro.
Parking possible near the church in the village centre or in the direction of Algar Seco.
Walking times: Carvoeiro – Algar Seco 20 min., Algar Seco – Praia de Vale de Santianes 50 min., Praia de Vale de Santianes – Carvoeiro 50 min.; total time 2 hr (5.5 km).

Ascent: 120 m of ascents and descents.
Refreshments: All categories of restaurants in Carvoeiro, beach bars in Algar Seco and on the Praia de Vale de Santianes.
Grade: Easy walk along rocky paths, trails and little-used roads
Alternative: At first, follow the description for Walk 12, then extend that leisurely stroll to a cliff ramble all the way to Benagil.

This ramble distils the Algarve's geological objects of interest into a compact package and also leads to one of the loveliest sandy bays to be found on this stretch of the coast. A break for a swim can also be taken.

Directly behind the church in **Carvoeiro**, a beaten path ascends to the edge of the coastal cliffs where we turn left along footpaths. 400 m on, descend along the steps to the right to visit the first fantastic caves and cliff formations. Returning to the cliff's edge, continue along the paths parallel to the coastal road for another 300 m. Now take the steps that descend into a bizarre world of shimmering, red through yellow-coloured rock arches and the grottoes of **Algar Seco**. In the centre of it all, the first break can be taken in the Café Boneca.

After admiring this geological spectacle, return to the edge of the cliff and turn right, heading east along paths with lovely views. 500 m on, reach the narrow beach of **Vale do Covo** below a »modern spectacle« – the Hotel Almansor.

The path now ascends steeply to a stretch of coastline boasting lush vegetation. After 1 km, descend to the narrow crescent beach of the marvellous **Praia de Vale de Santianes**, hidden beneath the overhanging cliffs and seashell crags.

»Seeing through things« in Algar Seco.

For the return route, we could retrace our way back along the same cliff paths or along the little-used tarmac road »Estrada Farol« running parallel. For the weary walker, bus service back to Carvoeiro is available along this road.

12 From Carvoeiro to Benagil

Grottoes, cliffs and beaches along a spectacular stretch of coastline

Carvoeiro – Praia do Carvalho – Benagil

Starting point: Carvoeiro, 50 m. Hourly bus service to Lagoa. By car: from Lagoa via the N 124-1 to Carvoeiro. Parking possible at the church.
Destination: Benagil, 10 m. By car: from the N 125 follow the sign, the turn-off is 2.5 km from either Lagoa and Porches. Parking possible at the restaurant »O Litoral« above the Praia de Benagil. Bus service between Carvoeiro and Club Atlantico along the coastal road running parallel.
Walking times: Carvoeiro – Praia do Carvalho 2½ hr, Praia do Carvalho – Benagil ½ hr; total time 3 hr (7.6 km).

Ascent: 200 m of ascents and descents.
Refreshments: Restaurants in Carvoeiro and Benagil, beach bars on many of the beaches along the way.
Grade: Moderately strenuous coastal walk along rocky cliff paths with short stretches along tarmac roads. A few steep ascents and descents.
Alternatives: 1. For the first leg, you can follow the route as described in Walk 11 to visit the Algar Seco. 2. The walk can be cut short by 1½ or 2½ hr by transferring to the coastal bus line with service to Farol or Algarve Club Atlantico (running 11 times a day).

The route embraces a few of the most beautiful and rarely visited beaches of this cliff-dominated stretch of coastline and offers jutting rocks overlooks with superb views. Our destination is the quiet fishing village of Benagil.
From the church in **Carvoeiro**, a path leads in a few metres to the cliff tops above the coastline and then turns left. 400 m as well as 700 m further on, pass by stepped trails that descend into the tangle of sea stacks and grottoes (see Walk 11). Continue along the cliff trail always heading towards the lighthouse of Alfanzina. The first steep descent and ascent along steps and

Trail marking: the »farol« of Alfanzina.

narrow paths lead after another 500 m by the Hotel Almansor through the **Vale de Covo** with a small inlet beach. Another short stretch continues along the hotel buildings above the coast until the broad trail swings left at the Hotel Cristal and keeps parallel to the Estrada Farol.

Our next goal is the **lighthouse (Farol) of Alfanzina**. After 300 m, ignore the right fork to Praia de Santianes and continue along the road for almost 1 km more until reaching the grand fountain at the Club Rocha Brava. At the road junction 200 m on, turn right to reach the *farol* – perched fully exposed on a cliff.

Behind the lighthouse and to the left, the cliff trail begins on the other side of an easily hopped fence and quickly becomes a steep path leading through a gorge that is somewhat troublesome to cross. On the other side, bear right to return to the cliff's edge and pick up either a path that is more direct but exposed, or one which keeps a respectful distance from the rim. After a kilometre of enjoying lovely views and with only slight ascents and descents, pass by the Algarve Club Atlantico (last bus stop for the line to Carvoeiro!) and then descend over steps to the little **Praia do Carvalho**.

For the final half hour, we can relax along a broad trail that ascends at the other end of the beach. Reach a hillock with pine trees and then follow along the coast while taking in some delightful views.

The next descent leads after not quite 1 km down to the quiet bay and the little fishing village of **Benagil**.

13 To the pilgrimage chapel Senhora da Rocha

Cliff top walk to bathing bays, sandy beaches and to the patron saint of fishermen

Benagil – Praia da Marinha – Senhora da Rocha – Armação de Pêra

Starting point: Benagil, 10 m. By car: signposted from the N 125, turnoff 2.5 km from either Lagoa or Porches. Parking possible at the restaurant »O Litoral« above the Praia de Benagil.
Destination: Armação de Pêra, 10 m. Bus station 300 m inland from the fort. By car: signposted after Alcantarilha on the N 125. Parking possible along the coast and at the Senhora da Rocha chapel.
Walking times: Benagil – Praia da Marinha ½ hr, Praia da Marinha – Senhora da Rocha 1 hr, Senhora da Rocha –

Armação de Pêra ¾ hr; total time 2¼ hr (8.7 km).
Ascent: 120 m of ascents and descents.
Grade: Easy walk along cliff top paths and trails.
Refreshments: Bars and restaurants in Benagil, at the Senhora da Rocha, in Armação de Pêra, as well as on all the beaches along the way.
Tipp: Porches, 4 km north-west of Armação de Pêra, is one of the Algarve's ceramic centres. The aquatic park paradise »The Big One« is also located here.

Benagil has kept the charm of a typical fishing village with seafood restaurants well worth a visit – a superb start for this spectacular tour. From the car park, do not take the little street all the way down to the bay, instead after a few metres and before the first left-hand bend and before the first restaurant on the left, turn off left to ascend along steps. Here a path begins and keeps bearing right, leading eventually to the coast. Continue on, keeping to the path closest to the coastline and which is marked the entire way with red and blue dots.

After 1 km, the path swings inland and crosses over the first shallow valley. Ascend steadily on and soon reach well-nigh fantastic cliff formations,

caves and blowholes, dropping all the way down to the ocean below. The Algarve coast just like in picture postcards!

As soon as we can break away from this phantasmagoria for the senses, we have only another 500 m to reach the next highlight. From the car park above the **Praia da Marinha**, a very lovely and well-constructed cobble-stone trail continues along the coastline and then, 200 m on, steps tempt us to »the Algarve's most beautiful beaches«. A good selection of beach bars also awaits us. Whether choosing a swimming break or not, to continue the walk, keep along the cobblestone trail that soon becomes less maintained. 500 m on, meet up with a wooden fence forewarning the dangers of falling from the sheer coastal cliffs. After another 300 m, cross again over a shallow valley and on the other side pick up a path leading back to the line of cliffs.

Still another small valley must be traversed before reaching the next re-splendent sandy beach in 1 km, the **Praia de Albandeira**. Climb up steps at the other end of the beach to reach the coastline trail. The skyline of Armação de Pêra appears to be quite near however, after 500 m, another deep valley must be crossed. Descend left bearing inland through under-growth and take the first chance to climb down to the valley floor along a steep path. Now head down the valley until reaching the beach; here two paths with red dot markings ascend to a trail that leads right and quickly re-turns to the cliff's edge. If you wish to take another break for a swim, take the steps to the right 500 m on to descend to Praia Senhora da Rocha. In no time at all, reach the chapel **Senhora da Rocha** picturesquely perched on a promontory. A path to the right leads to the shrine, to the left, more worldly pleasures are waiting in the bar/restaurants. Especially noteworthy in the simple little church built in the 16th century are the columns that most likely originate from a Roman temple. For the last leg of the route, continue on with the chapel at our backs, crossing the car park and along the tarmac road for a while. In front of the Hotel Viking, ascend right along steps to the seaside promenade.

This stretch of the coastal route leads almost 2 km along the hotel complex Vila Vita until reaching the car park by the Hotel do Levante. Here bear right to finally descend along steps to the Hotel Garbe on the west end of the beach where a lovely gardened promenade be-gins. The old village centre of Armação de Pêra on the east end between the fishermen's beach and the fort maintains a certain charm and is well worth a visit.

14 From Armação de Pêra to Albufeira

Along the coastal path crossing numerous coves and along the cliff formations near Albufeira

Armação de Pêra – Praia da Galé – Praia do Castelo – Albufeira

Starting point: Armação de Pêra, 10 m. Bus station 300 m inland from the fort. By car: signposted past Alcantarilha on the N 125. Best to park on the eastern end of the coastal road.

Destination: Albufeira, 10 m. Bus station in the village centre in the Av. de Liberdade. By car: signposted starting from the IP 1 and the N 125. Parking possible along the streets leading into the centre.

Walking times: Armação de Pêra – Praia da Galé 1 hr, Praia da Galé – Praia do Castelo ¾ hr, Praia do Castelo – Albufeira 1½ hr, total time 3¼ hr (15.4 km).

Ascent: 150 m.

Grade: Easy walk along a firm sandy beach and sometimes rocky cliff paths.

Refreshments: Bars and restaurants at the starting point and destination as well as on every beach along the route.

Tips: The view from the overlook situated to the east above the city beach and the Dolphin show in the Zoomarine Park near Guia are worth seeing.

After crossing broad sandy beaches, the coastal path twists and turns in constant undulating walking, opening lovely views as it passes from bay to bay. In-between, towering sandstone cliffs in ever-changing variation as well as verdant pine groves and a diverse spectrum of water-worn valleys – the Algarve straight out of picture postcards!

An outstanding starting point for this walk is the old fortress with the **Santo Antonio chapel** above the fishermen's harbour at the eastern end of the coastal road at **Armação de Pêra**. The start of our route can clearly be seen: the coastline to the east along the harbour. After half an hour along the sandy beach, the mouth of the lagoon and the **Ribeira de Espiche** presents an obstacle easy to cross by wading.

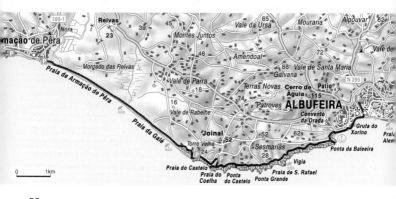

Ascent from the Praia da Gale.

Behind the beach bar at Galé, a distinct path marked with red dots and hugging the coastline lures us into the diverse world of the coastal cliffs. Not quite 2 km after setting out on the cliffs and past a short stretch of pine woods, the path merges into a tarmac road. Follow this to the right and continue until reaching the gate to an access road; turn right here and descend to the pleasant sandy bay **Praia do Castelo** surrounded by cliffs.

Where the tarmac road ends, a path begins left leading above bizarre sandstone crags and crossing through an apartment complex with pretty flowering plants. After 750 m, steps lead down to **Praia da Coelha** with a narrow sandy beach and yet another beach bar. Above this inlet and 100 m to the left, a post marked with a red dot lures us to the right and to an especially spectacular stretch in our route. At first, continue along the coastline passing bizarre cliffs. Not quite 1 km on, reach the next dusty road, descending to the inlet **Praia de São Rafael**. Paths to the right tempt us through little water-eroded valleys.

Unfortunately, this splendour comes to an end after another 1.5 km. A construction site spill, reaching all the way to the edge of the cliff, blocks the coastal path, forcing us to ascend left to a dusty road. Later this turns into a tarmac road that we follow to the right ending at the overlook on the **Ponta da Baleeira**. The immense new marina below us blocks the direct route to **Albufeira**. First we must skirt around this by climbing down over the slope then along a little street before picking up the Rua L. Coelho to descend to the beach that is our goal. To reach the bus stop, cross through the tunnel to Rua 5 de Outubro and take this to the right only to immediately turn left on the Av. da Liberdade.

15 From Albufeira to Olhos de Agua

Along the rugged, broken cliff coastline to delightful bathing bays

Albufeira – Praia da Oura – Praia da Balaia – Olhos de Agua

Starting point: Albufeira, 10 m. Bus station. By car: signposted starting from the IP 1 and the N 125. Parking possible along the streets leading to the centre.
Destination: Olhos de Agua, 10 m. Station for the bus line Albufeira – Falésia on the main road 1 km north of the beach. By car: from Albufeira towards Quarteira, past the Vale Navio turn right. Parking possible directly at the beach.
Walking times: Albufeira – Praia da Oura

1¼ hr, Praia da Oura – Praia da Balaia ¾ hr, Praia da Balaia – Olhos de Agua ½ hr; total time 2½ hr (8.7 km).
Ascent: 50 – 150 m depending on the route conditions.
Grade: Easy walk along cliff paths and over stretches of sandy, sometimes rocky, beach.
Refreshments: At the starting point and destination numerous restaurants. Bars and cafés on all the beaches en route.

A marvellous walk, always keeping to the seashore – but only possible 3 hours before and after low tide! All along this route, the ocean presents us with the tangy smell of sea air and a multitude of lovely spots for swimming. At high tide, the sea encroaches upon the enticing routes along the cliffs, making these impassable and leaving only the beaches free of tidewater. For the »bathing walker«, who spent too long a time romping in the waves, trails heading inland and to a nearby bus stop can be taken at every beach.

From the bus station in **Albufeira's centre**, follow the Av. da Liberdade south direction to Largo Eng. Duarte Pacheco, one of the prettiest, flower-adorned squares in the town. Turn right here and after a few metres, turn left in the Rua 5 da Outobro. The pedestrian tunnel brings us to the beach. Here, turn left following the seashore east. During low tide, walk to

Only possible at low tide: the seashore walk at Olhos de Agua.

the other side of the old fishermen's harbour and then continue below the cliffs. Otherwise, ascend the steps to the left climbing to Rua G. Coutinho. Follow this to the rest-cure home INATEL then descend right to the sandy beach **Praia dos Alemanos**. The looming, sheer rock face cliffs below the **Forte S. João** can easily be skirted around in 2 km by climbing the concrete steps left. A panoramic path follows, heading above the rocky cliffs until descending over steps after 600 m down to the sandy inlet **Praia da Oura**.

To skirt around the next cliffs, scramble over rocks that can only be used during low tide. Follow the coastline for 1 km to **Praia da Balaia** on the other side of the next cape. The appellation discloses the fact that in this peaceful inlet, beached whales have met their fate. The route ahead changes between stretches of rocks and the sandy beach Praia de Maria Luisa until reaching the quaint little fishermen's harbour **Olhos de Agua** below the next set of cliffs. The peculiar attraction of the sandy beach for this relatively tourist-oriented village lies in the fresh water springs that are only visible during low tide.

16 From Olhos de Agua to Praia da Falésia

Leisurely circular route to one of the Algarve's most beautiful expanses of beach

Olhos de Agua – Alfamar – Olhos de Agua

Starting point and destination: Olhos de Agua, 10 m. Station for the bus line Albufeira – Falésia on the main road 1 km north of the beach. By car: from Albufeira towards Quarteira, past the Vale Navio turn right. Parking possible at the beach.
Walking times: Olhos de Agua – Hotel Alfamar ¾ hr, Alfamar – Olhos de Agua

1 hr, total time 1¾ hr (7.6 km).
Ascent: 70 m.
Grade: Easy walk over sandy beaches and along cliff paths.
Refreshments: Restaurants in Olhos de Agua, at the barranco do Bilheiro as well as on some of the beaches and at the Hotel Alfamar.

This leisurely coastal walk embraces the beauty of one of the most noteworthy landscapes in the Algarve – the kilometre-long, still mostly undeveloped cliff coastline of the Praia da Falésia. Stunning beaches combine with white and colourful cliffs, in addition to deep green, pine-spotted valleys that lure the walker to extra excursions.

Our starting point and destination is the sandy beach of the pretty fishing village **Olhos de Agua**. Coming from the bus stop, turn left and head east. Before and after low tide, we can skirt around the jutting promontory that cuts off the beach by scrambling over the rocks near the waterline. If the tidewater is too high, ascend left along the distinct path, climbing up the dunes and, on the other side, descend steeply to the seemingly never-ending seashore. The firm sand presents a pleasant surface for the gentle route which keeps along the water's edge. Even when the barranco do Bilheiro, only some metres further on, tempts us with its wild greenery, we should save this excursion for the return route.

Near the **Praia da Aldeia das Açoteias**, an access road lures masses of bathers to the sea and to a restaurant. Soon after, the Hotel Alfamar, somewhat set back from the seashore, can be picked out by the beach equipment presented here.

In front of the Hotel Alfamar, turn left, ascend along a path to climb the cliffs and then turn immediately left onto a distinct path. The panoramic return route strides high above the ocean, opening new insights into the coastal landscape and superb views reaching from Faro to Albufeira. After some ascents and descents, cross over the road to Aldeia das Açoteias.

On the other side of the access road, the path leading along the cliffs is sometimes so inhibited by the golf course that it is better to switch back to the more reliable beach route. After a good 2 km reach the mouth of the broad Barranco do Bilheiro. Along a fortified trail, cross over this pine-green valley to the right and head north. At its end and after another 1 km, meet up with a tarmac road. Turn left to reach the first houses and continue on to the **Olhos de Agua**'s centre.

The cliffs at the Praia da Falésia.

17 Along the Praia da Falésia to Praia da Rocha Baixinha

A fabulous, secluded stretch of the cliff coastline is thoroughly explored

Alfamar – Praia da Rocha Baixinha – Vilamoura – Alfamar

Starting point and destination: Hotel Alfamar, 10 m. Last bus stop for the line Albufeira – Falésia. By car: from Albufeira towards Quarteira, past the Vale Navio turn right towards Olhos de Agua, then left towards Rocha Baixinha, afterwards turn right to the Hotel Alfamar; parking possible here.

Walking times: Alfamar – Rocha Baixinha – Vilamoura 1½ hr, Vilamoura – Alfamar 1¾ hr; total time 3¼ hr (12.3 km).

Ascent: 40 m.

Grade: Easy walk along a firmly-packed sandy beach and along cliff paths.

Refreshments: There are seaside restaurants near the Hotel Alfamar, a kiosk in Rocha Baixinha, bar/restaurants in Vilamoura.

Tip: The ruins of the Roman settlement on the harbour at Vilamoura.

This less demanding circular route touches on one of the Algarve's most beautiful stretches of seashore: the almost completely undeveloped Praia da Falésia, with many cliffs and bordered to the east by the Praia da Rocha Baixinha. Numerous sandy beaches along the route invite the walker to a refreshing dip in the sea.

Starting at the **Hotel Alfamar**, head for the beach and then turn left following along the packed sand of the seashore and heading east. Sweeping away before us to the left, the shimmering multi-coloured coastal cliffs are sliced by green valleys covered with pine trees. To the right, the wide-open sea

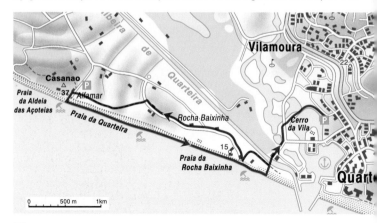

and straight ahead in the distance, you can spot a lighthouse: the *farol* at Faro. A backwards view stretches all along the cliff coastline seawards from Albufeira. After a good 3 km when the cliffs gradually reduce in height and the sand becomes softer making the walk more tiring, a kiosk appears before us to the left among the dunes: our first goal – the **Praia da Rocha Baixinha**. Turn left inland to reach the river – **Ribeira de Quarteira**. Cross the river over the footbridge. Cut across the car park and follow the narrow street skirting left around the harbour basin. Take the next road to the right that heads towards the high-rises of Vilamoura to finally reach **the yacht harbour Aldeia do Mar** with a good selection of restaurants and bars to take a break. The return route retraces the approach until reaching the river crossing. Just before arriving at the beach, turn right onto a trail into the dunes to reach the white house of the customs officer. Here turn right onto the panoramic trail above the cliffs towering higher and higher as we go. When a little airport appears before us, turn left to skirt around it and continue above the sea. Not much further on, the path descends to the car park in front of the **Hotel Alfamar** and the last stop of the bus line.

The nearly endless view at the Praia da Falésia.

18 From Vilamoura to Faro's beach

From the end of the coastal cliffs to the unspoilt fishing village on the Ilha de Faro

Vilamoura/Aldeia do Mar – Quarteira – Vale do Lobo – Quinta do Lago – Ilha de Faro

Starting point: Vilamoura (or Quarteira), 10 m. Bus service to Faro, Loulé and Albufeira. By car: both towns can be approached from the N 125 via signposted roads. Parking possible in Vilamoura at the yacht harbour, in Quarteira on the eastern village limits near the seaside promenade.
Destination: Ilha de Faro, 10 m. Bus service to Faro. By car: from the EN 125 from Faro turn off towards the airport. Continue as signposted to Ilha de Faro. Parking possible on the other side of the bridge.

Walking times: Vilamoura – Quarteira ½ hr, Quarteira – Vale do Lobo ¾ hr, Vale do Lobo – Quinta do Lago ¾ hr, Quinta do Lago – Ilha de Faro 1¼ hr; total time 3¼ hr (16.4 km).
Ascent: None.
Grade: Easy, but at the end, somewhat of a plod along sometimes soft stretches of sand.
Refreshments: Restaurants in Vilamoura, Quarteira and Ilha de Faro, beach bars in Vale do Lobo and Quinta do Lago.
Tip: Faro, the Algarve's ancient capital, deserves more than just a fleeting visit.

Our starting point is the Hotel Atlantis in the village centre of Vilamoura/Aldeia do Mar with its huge high-rises and immense harbour. A wooden walkway leads to the beach where we turn left to head for Quarteira.
Quarteira, the first stop on our walk, has managed to shake off its reputation as the Algarve's »drug haven«. After passing through the colourful collection of huts, end up on a promenade running straight along a superb sandy beach. At low tide, walk easily and leisurely on the packed sand at

In the lagoon landscape of the Ria Formosa.

the water's edge. At high tide, take the cliff path through the dunes. Now walk for a while along the green pine landscape of the golf courses at Vale do Lobo. To our left, the chain of cliffs and dunes level out gradually as we walk. Far in the distance, our goal appears before us: the coastal settlement in front of Faro. A good 7 km past Quarteira, a wooden walkway attracts us left. From the top of the dunes, enjoy the first view overlooking the lagoon habitat of the bird sanctuary **Parque Natural da Ria Formosa**, stretching far to the east of Faro. Shame on the walker who disturbs the birds here! On the other side of the lagoon, arise luxury hotels, fantastic golf courses and green pine groves – the pictorial park landscape of Quinta do Lago.

Somewhat taxing is the nearly 5 km final stretch over loose sand. It seems that we will never reach the houses at the **Praia de Faro**. Finally arrive at the limits of the fishing settlement and a concrete-paved trail provides an easy crossing. In the centre of the beach town some bars and restaurants await the parched walker. The bus stop is located on the other side of the bridge.

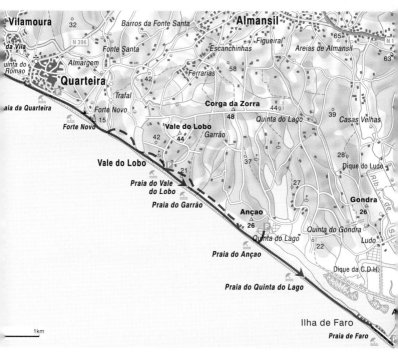

The Sotavento Coast (Eastern Algarve)

It appears that only a handful of visitors to the Algarve are aware that another coastline exists to the east of Faro. The Portuguese call this area stretching to the Spanish border – the *Sotavento*, the coast facing away from the wind. The Parque Natural da Ria Formosa with its islands and a vast tidewater habitat frequented by diverse species of wetland birds also offers seemingly endless and level sandy beaches that are often only accessible by boat. Not until reaching Manta Rota does this tideland complex come to an end. The Sotavento is quieter in every respect when compared to the rugged and changeable but also thoroughly tourist-oriented Barlavento coast. Tavira with its tranquil ambience, sleepy fishing ports and tiny beach settlements on the outlying island as well as the almost worldly chequerboard city Vila Real de Santo António – everything belongs somehow to the ancient but still intact realm of the fisherman and the farmer.

For this section, leisurely walks along the broad beaches are presented in four routes. They begin with the coastal paths of the Barlavento walks and extend these almost without a break all the way to the river border of Spain, the Rio Guadiana. Accommodation available in Olhao, Fuseta, Pedras del Rei, Santa Luzia, Tavira, Cabanas, Manta Rota, Vila Nova de Cacela, Monte Gordo, Vila Real de Santo António as well as on the islands of Armona and Culatra make it possible to undertake a complete long-distance trek from Faro to Vila Real.

Sand galore by Manta Rota.

Pirate nest in bygone years – Cacelha Velha.

19 Ilha da Culatra

An island walk into the past

Culatra – Leuchtturm – Culatra

Starting point and destination: Culatra, 5 m. Only reachable by boat from Olhao (several trips are offered daily). Olhao has both bus and rail connections to Faro.
Walking times: Culatra – lighthouse ¾ hr, return ¾ hr, total time 1½ hr (8.6 km).
Ascent: Not worth mentioning.
Grade: Easy beach walk; only during high

tide can the walk along the dunes over soft sand become more strenuous.
Refreshments: In Culatra and at the lighthouse.
Alternative: Since the boats also put in at the lighthouse (*farol*), the return can be made from there, saving the backtrack along the length of the island.

Culatra is the smallest and the most distant of the barrier islands in the Ria Formosa Natural Park. The remoteness of this fishing village on the Ilha da Culatra helps maintain a certain »world's end« ambience that can transport an attentive and sensitive visitor back to a time when fishing and not tourism was the mainstay of existence for all of the coastal settlements in the Algarve. The island's own school and church support the impression of »splendid isolation«. The better part of the island is enclosed by a barbed wire fence – a military manoeuvre zone that is fortunately seldom used.

The distant Ilha da Culatra.

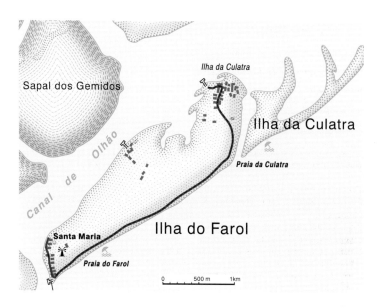

We begin the walk after embarking on the island (first the boat puts in at Culatra, then at Farol) by taking a leisurely ramble through the colourful world of the little fishermen's huts. Now with our backs to the village, head left to the seaside beach and walk along here for a good 4 km to reach the lighthouse, a target that cannot be missed on this one-time separate island of Ilha do Farol.

Apart from enjoying a languid swim in the delightfully pristine waters, you must be sure to take an excursion into the dunes, especially in springtime. The vegetation here is made up of stubby but lushly-blooming bushes and flowers, an appealing contrast to the bright, shimmering sand.

Some summer houses cluster around the lighthouse. When the lighthouse keeper arrives to take his watch in the evening, you can accompany him up the tower to enjoy the distant views over the entire coastal world of the Algarve as well as far into the hinterland.

The return route back to Culatra village follows the seaside as well.

Some private over-night accommodation is even offered here, in case you missed the last boat due to an over-abundance of delighted gaping – or if you dare to make a longer escape to the smallest inhabited island in the Algarve.

20 On the Ilha da Armona

A tideland walk to the bathing island of Olhao

Bias do Sul – Ilha da Armona – circular walk on the island – Bias do Sul

Starting point: The car park south of Bias do Sul, 10 m, or 2 km to the east, the railway station at Fuseta on the Faro – Tavira line. By car: from the N 125 take the turn-off to Bias do Sul. After 400 m, turn right onto a track. 400 m further on, turn left. Parking possible at the railway crossing.

Walking times: Car park – Ilha da Armona ¼ hr, Ilha da Armona – Praia da Armona 1 hr, circular walk 1 to 3 hr, Praia da Armona – car park 1¼ hr; total time 2½ to 5½ hr (15 to 23 km).

Ascent: None.

Refreshments: Beach bar on the Praia da Armona (there is a campsite nearby where wooden bungalows can also be rented) and on the Praia da Fuseta.

Grade: Easy walk along trails/paths crossing the island and through the tideland; no permanent path at the water's edge.

Alternative: Regular ferry service from Praia da Armona to Olhao and from Praia da Fuseta to Fuseta – especially recommended as an alternative to the starting point / destination, e.g. during high tide.

Tip: Circular walk through the Centro de Educação Ambiental de Marim in Ria Formosa Natural Park (about 2 hr, 4.5 km). Open from 9 a.m. – 12.30 p.m./ 2 p.m. – 5.30 p.m., approach by car along the N 125. 1.5 km east of Olhao, follow the signs for »Parque Natural/ campground«; after 500 m, turn right and cross the railway tracks. The entrance is 50 m on to the left. The circular route embraces about 20 stops along the ecosystem of the lagoon and presents the economic value of the location. You can experience, for example, a tide mill, mussel banks, a tuna-fishing boat and salt works. A highlight is the »Cao del Agua«, a race of giant poodles renowned for their swimming abilities.

An island, beach and tideway walk where every walker can decide how far he wants to go. On the deserted beach and in the dunes on the Ilha da

Pathless along the seashore.

Armona, a quiet place can always be found to rediscover time and space on your own. The route between the car park and the island embraces a tideway realm teeming with wetland birds. The passage is only secure for 3 hours before and after low tide.

Begin the walk at the car park and cross over the tracks of the Faro – Tavira railway line following a trail through the tidelands that soon swings right and then left heading for the island. Once reaching the sandy island, turn right. Along a dirt trail, sometimes through sparse stands of pine and eucalyptus, reach the west end of the island after 3 km. The ruins of a former customs office is a reminder of a time when smuggling was one of the main sources of income for the inhabitants. Here is also the broadest beach of the island, a self-serve restaurant and the landing for boats to Olhao.

If you desire even more island solitude, take the trail that at first follows the coastline south and then turns east after a good 1 km. After 7 km, reach the handful of buildings on the **Praia da Fuseta**. Not quite another 2½ km, reach the east end of the Ilha da Armona on the **Barra da Fuseta**. During the return walk and after 3.5 km (or at the fourth sand cliff past the Praia da Fuseta) you really should turn to the right and venture, at first pathless, into the dunes. In the spring, the dunes are blanketed in yellow and white flowering camomile and purple sea pink.

Soon meet up with a broader path that becomes a trail leading left at first then turning right to merge into the approach trail which at low tide crosses over the dry tideway. Through the ever-changing tideland, finally return to the car park. During high tide, it is better to use the boat service described above to ferry over to Olhao or Fuseta and safely return to the mainland. In case there is a lack of suitable walking trails along the tideland seashore, the return trip must be made by private vehicle or taxi.

21 On the Ilha de Tavira

Infinite walking for pleasure at sea level

Pedras del Rei – Praia do Barril – Praia das Cascas – Arraial do Livramento – Praia do Barril – Pedras del Rei

Starting point and destination: Pedras del Rei, 5 m. Bus service to Tavira, railway station Santa Luzia on the Faro – Tavira line 1.5 km away. By car: signposted from the N 125. Parking possible at the shore.
Walking times: Pedras del Rei – Praia do Barril ¼ hr, Praia do Barril – Praia das Cascas 1¼ hr, Praia das Cascas – Arraial do Livramento 2½ hr, Arraial do Livramento – Praia do Barril 1¼ hr, Praia do Barril – Pedras del Rei ¼ hr; total time

5½ hr (22.5 km).
Ascent: Almost no ascents or descents.
Grade: Easy beach walk along firm or soft sand depending on the tides.
Refreshments: Bar/restaurants in Praia do Barril and Praia the Cascas.
Alternatives: The walk can be cut short by returning by boat from the Praia das Cascas directly to Tavira or by not taking the excursion to Arraial do Livramento and back.

For the walker who wishes to enjoy the virtually endless expanses of the secluded sandy beaches in the Sotavento to his heart's content, this wish will certainly be granted on the largest of the barrier islands. Not long after leaving the crowded beaches behind him, the walker finds himself alone with the ocean, the wind, the wild birds and his own spirit. Time and again, the soft, warm and smooth expanses of sandy beach beckon for a dip in the azure sea.

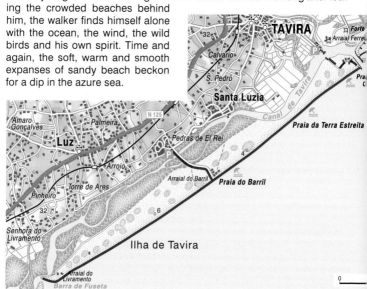

At the island's end – Praia das Cascas.

Begin at the banks of the tideway in **Pedras del Rei** and cross over the pontoon footbridge. If you prefer to give your legs a little rest, on the other side of the bridge and right out of a children's book, a narrow gauge railway train is waiting to take you for a ride along the first kilometre. Also on foot, this first stretch along inlaid plates is quite pleasant and often shaded by trees and bushes.

In **Praia do Barril**, on the other side of the dunes, we are not only lured by the flat sandy beach but also by two restaurants converted »tastefully« from the former coast guard station. Afterwards, turn left to follow the open beach for a good 5 km. You can take a little excursion into the dunes to wonder at the two »menhirs« there or to enjoy the views of the settlements along the tideland coast and in the distant hills. Otherwise, this walk does not offer many thrills – just enough free space to let the soul swing and sway along the way.

Before long, reach the **Praia das Cascas**, directly at the entrance to **Tavira**'s harbour – a few bar/restaurants, a little copse of trees and regular boat service to Tavira; here, you could call it a day for the »island of your dreams«. The trail to **Arraial do Livramento** presents the longest island walk in the Algarve. 12 km must be reckoned with from the east to the west end of the island. The question concerning the ferry option from Arraial do Livramento to Fuseta has just been pooh-poohed. There seems to be no other choice but to return along the 7 km to **Praia do Barril**. Well, look here! The little train awaits us, offering a chance to give our legs a rest, at least for the last kilometre. Over the swaying pontoon bridge – now we are back on dry land.

22 From Cabanas to Monte Gordo

Along the incomparable sandy beaches of the Sotavento with an excursion to Cacela Velha – bathed in history

Cabanas – Praia das Cabanas – Praia de Cacela – Cacela Velha – Praia de Manta Rota – Praia Verde – Monte Gordo

Starting point: Cabanas (Conceição's beach town), 5 m. Bus service to Tavira. Railway station 2 km away in Conceição. By car: from the N 125 follow the signs for Conceição and Cabanas. Parking possible in Cabanas near the ferry boat wharf for the peninsula.

Destination: Monte Gordo, 5 m. Bus service to Vila Real and Tavira. Railway station 1.5 km from the beach.

Walking times: Cabanas – Praia das Cabanas ¼ hr, Praia das Cabanas – Praia de Cacela 1 hr, Praia de Cacela – Cacela Velha ¾ hr, Cacela Velha – Praia de Manta Rota ½ hr, Praia de Manta Rota – Praia Verde ¾ hr, Praia Verde – Monte Gordo ¾ hr; total time 4 hr (19.2 km).

Ascent: 50 m of ascents and descents.

Grade: During low tide: easy walk mostly along broad sandy beaches and paths. At high tide, the walker must swing inland to the soft sands of the dunes, making the walk more arduous and time-consuming.

Refreshments: Numerous bar/restaurants at the starting point and destination as well as on the beaches en route and in Cacela Velha.

Alternative: Especially in low season, it can be difficult to arrange boat transfer from Cabanas to Praia the Cabanas on the peninsula. Another possibility for the walk is to start from Cacela Velha. Fábrica (located between Conceição and Cacela Velha) offers a possible place to arrange for a fishing boat to ferry you to the peninsula. This cuts the tour short by ½ hr.

Tip: The chequerboard town of Vila Real de S. António is worth a visit.

Not only the seemingly endless beaches of fine sand make this shadeless, level walk along the Sotavento coast so attractive. At Cacela Velha, we visit one of the Algarve's most remarkable and oldest fortresses, serving for a long time as the base of operations for pirates and smugglers. The route to this towering monument high above the seaboard also embraces the fully disparate, much more lush and colourful vegetation of the tideland side.

During high season, numerous boats ply back and forth from **Cabanas** to the offshore islands but even in low season, you can usually arrange a crossing by inquiring in one of the bar/restaurants along the shoreline road. Often at low tide, you can even reach the peninsula on foot. Once there, only a few strides over the dunes bring you to the spacious beach at the ocean side and for your first swim.

At the beach, turn left (staunch coastal walkers may choose to swing to the right – depending on the tide – and head for Barra de Tavira) and always follow the shoreline eastward. A good 2 km of beach walking then reach the »Barra do Lacém« which must be negotiated, but have no fear! – »barra« means »sandbank«. Only during high tide is there a danger of getting your feet wet.

Cacelha Vela enthroned over the lagoon.

Not quite 5 km later, reach **Cacela's beach** which also has ferry service to the »mainland«. Continue following the beach for another good 2 km until the inlet ends to the left. Here, cross over the beach and the dunes by heading inland and then meet up with a large car park on the western end of the apartment complex of Manta Rota. Now turn left along a sandy path running along the inland side of the dunes. Our »distant goal« Cacela Velha can be clearly seen.

Our nearest goal, however, is a white cubist house to the right and above the second set of dunes. At a fork in the trail 100 m on, bear right and immediately after turn right onto a path crossing through a natural depression. After 400 m, bear right once again and 100 m on, reach the edge of a field directly beneath the white house. Another 100 m further, turn left along an embankment only to leave this again 20 m on by turning right.

Continue walking along the floor of an inlet that has been drained dry. Fields lie above and to the right; to the left, the muck and mire of the lagoon hardly tempts us to take a dip. 200 m on, cross over a low dune to the right. After another 700 m, pass a »noria«, a typical Arabic-style well.

Meet up with a stream 500 m on – our last hurdle – and easily cross this by bearing left. Soon we are standing at the foot of the little fortress at **Cacela Velha**. Ascend along a path to the right then turn left along steps to reach the village square with an old Moorish well. It's like time-travelling back to past centuries as you ramble between the ancient buildings towards the Renaissance church.

Superb views encompass the offshore peninsula where we just walked, as well as all along the coast as far as Tavira to the west and the hotel high-rises of Monte Gordo, our destination to the east. The fortress is no longer the haunt of pirates and smugglers as it was in days gone by. On the contrary, the military personnel who resides here now, attempts to keep such rabble in check. A sight-seeing tour is not permitted.

For the route ahead (or as the starting point for the Alternative walk) retrace your steps along the path, descend to the right beneath the fortress, then cross the stream to the left.

For those who start the walk at Cacela Velha the route goes as follows: after 600 m pass by the old well, bear right 700 m further on and cross over the low dune. 300 m later, continue along the flat-topped dyke then turn left and immediately after, turn right (do not ascend left to the white, cubist house!).

After 200 m of walking along a field, turn right through thick undergrowth then continue steadily straight ahead aiming for the bulky building of the Hotel Altura. Reach the car park near the **Praia de Manta Rota** after 2.5 km and on the other side of the dunes, another marvellous bathing beach awaits us.

To enjoy, however, what is considered the most beautiful beach in the eastern Algarve – the **Praia Verde** – another 3 km of beach must be walked, passing by the »belle époque hotel« Altura. Ornamental umbrella pines sporting thick green topiary stretch almost to the beach. The little bar/restaurant here has also been highly praised.

The final few kilometres along the beach become overshadowed by the looming pyramid-formed hotel high-rises: Monte Gordo's landmark. As a compensation, this »hotel village« offers tourists just about anything imaginable, all the way up to a gambling casino. To reach the railway station on the other side of the N 125, turn left along the bustling main street.

The end of the lagoon: view from Cacelha Velha.

The west coast, the hinterland of Lagos and the Monchique hills

»The Wild West of the Algarve« – this appellation characterizes a spectrum of natural landscapes that differ from one another in many ways; these are collected together in ten walks. We cross through areas that seem light-years away from the tourist centres of the southern coast but only a few kilometres actually separate the quietude here from the hurly-burly over there.

Astonishingly solitary, wild and rugged is the image presented by the west coast. Astonishingly intact is the agricultural makeup of the villages and towns in the hinterland of Lagos. It is also astonishing that despite centuries of ruinous exploitation for the construction of sea-going galleys, vast stretches of deciduous forest in the Mata de Barão are still intact to provide plenty of shade for walkers today. A special treat is offered by the Barragem da Bravura, a fresh water reservoir surrounded by eucalyptus forests.

The pinnacle of surprises however, is found in the Serra de Monchique. Walks lead us along austere, thickly-wooded slopes to isolated villages and to panoramic heights, to the Algarve's highest summits: the Fóia and the Picota. The town of Monchique itself and, even more so, Caldas de Monchique amaze us with relics of a pilgrim and spa »tourism« that has lasted for over five hundred years.

Those of you who have taken a fancy to the west coast will want to while away some more time here along a coastal footpath that offers numerous possibilities for walking. Overnight accommodation can be found in Vila Nova de Milfontes, Almograve, Zambujeira, Odeceixe, Aljezur, Vale da

The grey cliffs of the west coast.

Leading walkers to the right way.

Telha, Arrifana, Espartal, Carrapateira and Vila do Bispo. In the hinterland of Lagos and in the Serra de Monchique lodging is offered in Barão de São João, Alcalar, Caldas de Monchique and Monchique.

23 To Torre de Aspa

A viewpoint and three of the most beautiful sandy beaches on the rugged western coast

Vila do Bispo – Torre de Aspa (156 m) – Praia do Castelejo – Praia da Cordama – Praia da Barriga – car park

Starting point and destination: Car park on the main road Vila do Bispo – Praia do Castelejo, 135 m. Bus service to Vila do Bispo. By car: from Vila do Bispo signposted »Castelejo«, car park to the right after 2.5 km.

Walking times: Car park – Torre de Aspa ¾ hr, Torre de Aspa – Praia do Castelejo ¾ hr, Praia do Castelejo – Praia da Cordama ½ hr, Praia da Cordama – Praia da Barriga ¼ hr, Praia da Barriga – car park 1¾ hr; total time 4 hr (17.6 km).

Ascent: 230 m of ascents and descents.

Grade: Because of a steep descent, a somewhat strenuous walk along broad trails and a sandy beach.

Refreshments: Beach bars in Praia do Castelejo and Praia da Cordama.

Alternatives: 1. From the beaches at Castelejo and Cordama, a return can be made along a road or along a track directly to the car park (for example, when high tide blocks the passage between the beaches).

2. If you begin the walk in Vila do Bispo, take a path running parallel to the road to the car park. Returning from the Praia da Barriga directly to Vila do Bispo bear left at the fork as described below and 150 m on at a junction continue straight ahead. 50 m later ascend to the left. Another 2 km on, turn right onto a path that meets up with the N 268 after 700 m. Turn right and you will soon arrive at a farmstead. Behind the farmstead, turn right to continue along a trail running parallel to the road for the last 1½ km until reaching Vila do Bispo.

Tip: The Matriz church in Vila do Bispo displays exquisite »azulejo« decoration, the surrounding and old village.

Is this the Algarve as well? 150 m high, sheer cliffs of black slate beaten by raging ocean waves, lonely highlands of heather where flowers of every colour bloom in the springtime, fragrant forests of pine and, snuggled in-between, kilometre long deserted beaches of dazzling sand.

A signboard at the car park, shaded by pines, gives an inkling of the trails awaiting us. Signposts lure us to the other side of the road and along a broad trail towards the first and highest point of the walk – the obelisk **Torre de Aspa**.

At first meander through sprawling pastureland and blankets of rock rose bushes blooming in springtime with thousands of white star-like flowers. The scenery changes to a colourful heath. The trail swings left skirting around a broad valley, passes by two houses and then swings right gradually. After 3.5 km past a weather station and following signs, turn right, skirt around the obelisk and after two left turns finally reach it in an approach from the northwest. The southernmost edge of Europe lies at our feet!

The viewpoint Torre de Aspa.

A chain of sandy beaches – a way and a destination.

Back along the approach route – now marked with blue dots and arrows – return in 150 m to the junction; turn right and at the fork 300 m on turn left, crossing through a mimosa wood towards a house. After another 1 km reach a promontory almost 150 m above the sea. The route heading north can be seen before us, sandy beach upon sandy beach all the way to the cone at Mirouco. From the tip of the promontory return to the house and then turn left onto a track that heads inland. Now walk one level kilometre through colourful heath until reaching a broad trail. Turn left to descend and continue in the same direction even after 500 m when the trail leads onto a narrow path along the ridge and descends steeply. This is the only difficult stretch of the tour. During the last drop in elevation, swing right to traverse the slope more on the level and to ease the descent into the dry valley. At the valley floor, follow the path left and seawards. Another 250 m to the right by scrambling over stones and rock, we finally find ourselves standing with sand underfoot on the splendid **Praia do Castelejo**.

After this steep descent, the route continues on the level. Only at low tide is it possible to scramble over rocks to the next sandy inlet, the **Praia da Cordama**, but not at high tide. The same is true for the passage to **Praia da Barriga** which seems, from a distance, impossible to negotiate. Sea spray marks the heavy pounding of the waves against the rock cone of Mirouco. Our beach route has come to an end. The walker yearning for more secluded beaches can only proceed »on the other side of the mountains«. We have reached the turnaround point of this tour.

Leave the beach behind by taking the dusty road. At the fork 150 m on, bear right (bearing left leads to the other beaches lying to the north). Now ascend for 1.5 km through a shady pine wood. Cross over a junction and continue straight on. 250 m later at a signpost for »Cordama«, turn right (the left track is an alternative route leading directly to Vila do Bispo). The narrow road winds along the slope through woods and heath to reach a fork in the trail after 2.5 km.

To the right is a possible descent to Praia da Cordama, to the left, a 1.2 km ascent to the merge of the tarmac road ascending from the Praia do Castelejo. After another 1.2 km heading up the valley, return to the car park on the high plain.

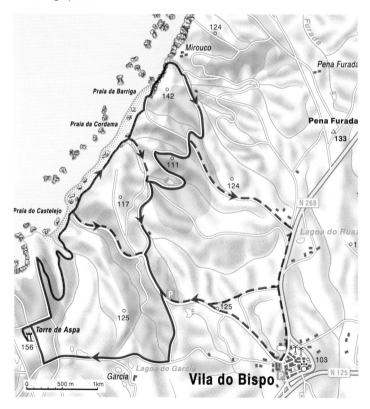

24 To the panoramic cliffs of Atalaia and Arrifana

Along the west coast trails to spectacular panoramic cliffs

Car park near Espartal – Ponta da Atalaia – Ponta da Arrifana – Vale da Telha – car park

Starting point and destination: Car park near Espartal, 85 m. By car: along the N 120 or the N 268 towards Aljezur. 1.5 km before Aljezur, turn left (sign »Valhe da Telha«); after 1 km, turn right. 5 km on: the beach settlement of Espartal; after ascending for 500 m, turn right; car park at a picnic place 200 m on after passing a left-hand bend. No bus service.

Walking times: Car park – Ponta da Atalaia ¾ hr, Ponta da Atalaia – Ponta da Arrifana 1 hr, Ponta da Arrifana – Vale da Telha ¾ hr, Vale da Telha – car park 1 hr; total time 3½ hr (15.9 km).

Ascent: 100 m of ascents and descents.

Grade: Level paths until Ponta da Atalaia then some strenuous ascents and descents along rocky paths; easy return route along little-used tarmac-paved and dusty roads.

Refreshments: Bar/restaurants on the Ponta da Arrifana and in the villages of Arrifana, Vale da Telha and Espartal.

Accommodation: Arrifana, Vale da Telha and Espartal.

Tip: The Moorish *castelo* above Aljezur and the narrow roads in the old little town are worth visiting.

When someone raves about the west coast and the fact that the ocean and scenery there is much more rugged, the flowers more colourful, the villages quieter and the beaches more secluded, then take him at his word – and also take the author's favourite west coast walk. In doing so, you will soon get to know and to love this area.

In springtime, it is a dream-like high walk a good 100 m above the raging sea and through an herb garden of thyme, lavender, sage and rosemary, between rock roses and all sorts of flowers blooming in a broad spectrum of colours. From the *Pontas* take in superb views and in Arrifana enjoy an easy to reach sandy beach. Already during the approach from Lagos through the cork oak forests of the Serra do Espinhaço de Cão, pass through a wondrous landscape. Curiosity aroused? Let's go!

Begin the walk to the right of the car park by turning to face the sea and climbing up the first panoramic cliff. Before us, to the left, we can see the end point of our initial route. Return to the car park and follow the dusty road 1 km south (the sea surges to our right). At the turnaround for this road, a sandy trail begins diagonally to the left and soon becomes a path while passing through the dunes.

From the many paths here, always choose the one nearest the coastline. Only after heavy periods of rainfall, we must to turn inland to skirt around two swampy areas. The level walk passes through an ever-changing dune landscape, curiously located here on the cliff top, with an astonishing ar-

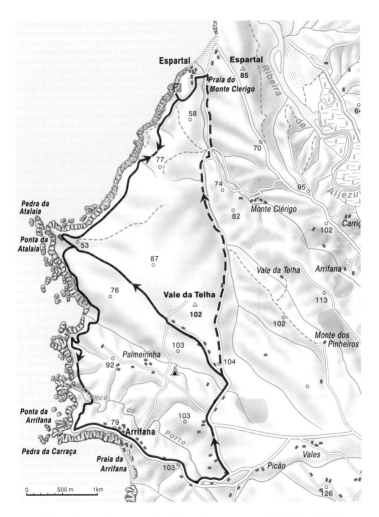

ray of flora. Our goal, crowned by the ruins of a concrete building is always in view ahead of us – **Ponta da Atalaia** – and can be reached without any effort.

Walking through flowering matos.

After taking in the fantastic views to the north and south, head for the next goal – the Ponta da Arrifana. Take the gravel road 150 m inland. Here, a distinct path turns right, crosses over a shallow valley and heads for the coastline. After 1 km cross over a dirt track then at a fork in the path 700 m on, bear right and keep parallel to the coastline. Now a steep descent follows, slippery underfoot, into a deep valley. After 300 m, at a level spot, cross the stream to the right over stepping stones. Head 20 m up the valley then begin an ascent traversing the slope and climbing to the top. The traces of paths merge here into the familiar coastal path.

Along the high plain, after 500 m, cross over a trail and then 20 m on at a fork, bear left and traverse a little shallow valley. After 250 m cross over a trailhead and 500 m further on, descend again into a natural depression. Another 500 m along the high plain – with a view to the left of modern settlements and a water tower – once again cross over a valley with a stream (the attractive rocky beach at the valley's end was visible from our path before).

Do not descend directly along the traces of paths straight to the stream but instead keep left, traversing the slope along a gradual descending path. In a left-hand bend, descend to the right into an idyllic little valley. Ascend right again and upon reaching the top, the panoramic cliff **Ponta da Arrifana** greets us.

The building that we saw before from so far away, turns out to be a long-awaited bar/restaurant! After taking our fill of the superb views from near and far (to the south, the Cabo de São Vicente can be spotted) continue left on the narrow road to reach the village limits in 250 m. Here more restaurants await us as well as a beach frequented by surfers, a fishermen's harbour far below and even accommodation in case the need arises.

If you want to continue the walk right away, reach the other end of the village after 1 km and then 500 m on, a junction; here turn left as signposted towards »Vale da Telha«. In a populated area of newly-built villas, we begin our roundabout route: after 1.5 km bear left then bear left again another kilometre further on, following the sign for the campground.

After passing the water tower on our left and another 800 m further on, we arrive at the surveyor's point and must choose our return route: the one turning left continues over two more roundabouts, always keeping straight on and then heads along a dusty road to return to Ponta da Atalaia. From there, continue along the familiar coastal trail to the car park.

Alternatively, we could carry on straight ahead, remain on the narrow tarmac road for 4 km and reach the fork onto the narrow dusty road that returns directly to the car park.

For those walkers who have some energy left: the pretty little town of Aljezur with a Moorish castle is worth a leisurely sight-seeing tour.

Our trail leads steadfast above the churning sea.

25 In the Mata Nacional de Barão de S. João

Forest trails rich in diversity passing through a relaxing woodland area

Circular walk around the Pedra Branca

Starting point and destination: The highpoint Pedra Branca, 178 m. By car: at the village limits from Lagos at the roundabout from the N 125 turn off onto the N 120 in the direction of Aljezur. Shortly before Bensafrim, turn left towards Barão de São João. 3.5 km on, at the village limits, turn right towards »Parque Merendas«/ »Mata Nacional«. After 300 m, ascend to the right along a dusty road. Parking possible at the highest point »Pedra Branca« (benches to the right).
Walking times: Circular walk 2 hr (7.7 km).
Ascent: 80 m.

Refreshments: Restaurant Florestal at the edge of Mata Nacional de Barão de S. João.
Grade: Easy walk along woodland trails.
Alternatives: Starting from the forest car park in the Parque de Merendas, a number of marked walking trails begin – including a fitness trail – that pass through shady eucalyptus and pine woods. In the log cabin at the village limits on the left-hand side of the road to the car park, walking guides and other information are available (Tuesdays–Sundays 10 a.m.–1 p.m.).
Tip: The Zoological Garden north of Barão de S. João is worth visiting.

Especially on hot summer days, the partially shady pine and eucalyptus forests of the Mata Nacional de Barão de S. João offer welcome relief. Along the route, when the walker thinks back to days gone by when these woods provided timber for the ships once used to discover far-away lands, then this is the perfect alternative to the clamour of beach life. Additionally, several cultural and historical attractions await us along the way.

A menhir from the Palaeolithic period is our first allurement. This is located 200 m left on the road that turns left before the white posts at the park exit. After this step back in time to prehistory, follow the blue-marked trail (with the car park to our backs, straight ahead), constantly providing sweeping

views to our right over the hilly farmland of the Algarve. After 1½ km, at a surveyor's point, another curiosity attracts us to the left of the trail »the rubble heap of Relva«.

Here, the visitor can let his fantasy take over. What stood on this site in days long past? A Roman fortress, or a medieval fairy-tale castle or an algarvian tower construction ...?

When the weather is clear, you can make out the southern coastline near Burgau and Luz in the distance. 3 km on, turn sharply left and then along many twists and turns pass through a sparse forest that only offers fleeting spots of shade. After bearing left twice more, finally return to the car park. On the way, we also passed the building Casa da Guarda and the little area of the Parque de Merendas (see Alternative).

Through thick and thin woods in flower.

26 On the Monte Novo

A surprising view from a craggy massif near Bensafrim

Bensafrim – Monte-Novo-summit (88 m) – the trail through almond groves – Bensafrim

Starting point and destination: Bensafrim, 45 m. Bus service to Lagos. By car: along the N 120 from Lagos towards Bensafrim, after 7 km and past the bridge, car park to the left of the road.

Walking times: Bensafrim – summit ½ hr, summit – trail through the almond groves 1½ hr, return to Bensafrim 20 min.; total time 2 hr 20 min (7.7 km).

Ascent: 120 m ascents and descents.

Grade: Short, easy walk along trails and paths.

Refreshments: Bar/restaurants in Bensafrim.

Important notice: Since summer 2004, construction work on the motorway could cause problems with the route or even make it impossible to walk.

This short walk, which can be undertaken as a pleasant excursion break while driving along the west coast, offers a double attraction. All year round you can enjoy a surprisingly sweeping view of the coast stretching from the south and over to the Monchique hills. In the spring (January through March) countless almond trees turn the countryside into the magical blooming »snow-covered« landscape of the legend.

Starting at the car park, walk along the N 120 back over the bridge then turn off to the right after 150 m along the N 535 towards Barão de São João. 200 m on, a narrow tarmac road turns off to the left; ascend along this to reach the **rocky plateau of the Monte Novo**. After another 200 m at a farm-

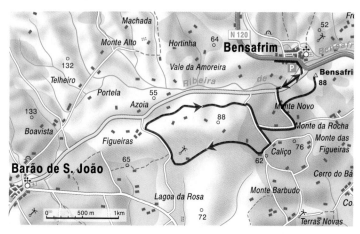

house, turn left onto a dirt trail and follow this through a charming terrain with fig, almond and olive trees. Already after a few paces and bearing left, we can make out in front of us the tarmac tower marking the **summit**.

To reach the tower, when the trail ends at a farmstead 200 m further on, turn left onto a path that surmounts numerous drystone walls bordering the fields. With our goal always in sight, we must negotiate a few hundred metres of unpleasant thorny bushes – long trousers are recommended – to reach our »victory column«.

The toil of our ascent is rewarded by a glorious view. Directly below us lies the village of Bensafrim and in the background across the hilly landscape, the mountains around Monchique reach to the sky. To the right, the hilly scenery around the Pedra Branca expands to block the view of the west coast beyond. When we turn around, enjoy a backwards view to Lagos and the rugged, ragged coastal regions.

The easiest return route retraces the ascent back to the tarmac road. Here, turn left and after 200 m turn right heading towards three farmhouses to reach these 250 m later. Turn left onto a path that ascends along numerous bends. Our destination is the ruins of a windmill perched atop a panoramic limestone ridge that we reach after a good 1.5 km. At a fork in the trail behind the mill, bear right following an old trail leading between stone walls and bearing further right. After a bend to the right and past a greenhouse, continue straight on to return to the three farmhouses 1.7 km later. Turn left here, descend and return along the approach route to **Bensafrim**.

A humble peak: the Monte Novo.

27 At the Barragem da Bravura

Through remote hills and eucalyptus forest to circle the reservoir

Dam – Torre da Guena – dam

Startingpoint and Destination: The dam of the Barragem da Bravura, 80 m. By car: from the N 125 in Odiáxere, turn off along the access road to »Barragem« (signposted). After 9 km, drive up to the viewpoint at the lake.
Parking possible next to the café or in front of the dam.
Walking times: Dam – Torre da Guena 2½ hr, Torre da Guena – dam 2½ hr; total time 5 hr (23.7 km).
Ascent: 300 m of ascents and descents; the alternative walk has 150 m of ascents and descents.
Grade: Easy but long walk via broad trails.
Refreshments: Café at the car park.
Alternative: The walk can be turned into a

panoramic circular walk. After 5.5 km, do not turn left, instead turn right into the valley. Now continue ascending for 1.3 km. After reaching the top, turn right onto another ascending trail. When the broad view to the right takes in the lake as well, two trails turn off to the right, one after the other. Ignore these trails and continue. 2 km after leaving the main walk our trail reaches the valley floor. Turn right here onto a trail descending through a wood and merge into the lake trail 500 m further on. Another 500 m to the left and we are standing again on the dam. The return route starting from the turnoff is not quite 1 hr.
Tip: Bathing is not allowed in the Barragem da Bravura.

This is a wonderful opportunity to trade the blazing summer heat of the Atlantic Coast for the cool, spicy air at the grand Bravura Reservoir. At first, the route follows partially shaded trails which later become exposed to the sun and then follows along the lakeside and through the wooded countryside as well as groves of olive trees.

Starting at the car park, a narrow road descends to the right ending at the dam which we cross over. Now continue for 3 km along the many arms of the reservoir. Time and again, paths tempt us to descend left to the shore but nevertheless we continue along the broad trail. We also ignore a broad trail ascending to the right after 500 m – the merging point for the alternative walk described above.

After 3 km of constantly changing views over the lake and of the hilly surroundings, begin an ascent to the right leaving the lake behind. The climb continues for 1.5 km through eucalyptus until reaching a junction where we turn left onto a descending trail. Along a wide bend to the right, continue on for over 500 m to reach the next fork in the trail. We recommend to take a diversion here (almost 2 km in total) descending to the left and leading to a viewpoint on the lake. Return to the fork, continue on straight ahead and descend 700 m in a wide left-hand sweep to a trail junction in the valley.

Here the alternative route turns right; our route ahead turns left following along the lake. This leads to the narrow and north-easternmost arm of the lake. On very sunny days, we recommend turning back here since the route

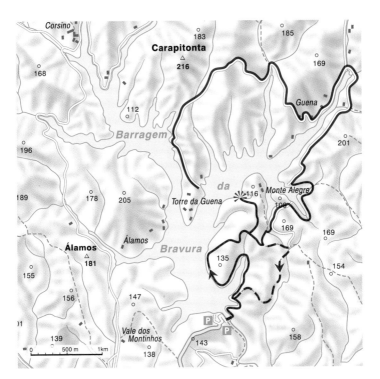

ahead leads (after crossing over the spot where the **Ribeira de Odiáxere** empties into the lake) in a sharp left-hand bend along the northern shore of the Barragem which is very exposed to the sun.

After 1 km, pass the handful of houses making up the hamlet of **Guena**. Here our trail turns right again, away from the lake, and over the next kilometre crosses the ridge of a hill. Past the next bridge crossing over one of the rivers feeding the lake, turn left along the lakeshore for a short stretch. Now the trail turns right again, leaving the lake behind and crosses over yet another hilltop. After another good 1.5 km, reach the reservoir once again. Along the last 2 km, walk at first above the lake then cross over a promontory to the left and finally reach the scattered houses of **Torre da Guena**.

Since swimming is not permitted in the reservoir, we can only return by retracing our steps back to the car park at the café.

28 In the Serra de Monchique

Gorge tour through the villages of the Algarve's highest hills

Casais – Monchique

Starting point: Casais, 280 m. Bus service to Monchique. By car: from the N 266 Portimão – Monchique 3 km beyond Caldas de Monchique, turn left onto the N 267. 5 km to Casais. Parking possible near the bus stop at the village limits.
Destination: Monchique, 420 m. Bus service to Portimão. See Walk 29.

Walking times: Casais – Monchique 2¾ hr (10.2 km).
Ascent: 180 m ascent.
Grade: Easy to moderate walk along woodland trails.
Refreshments: In Monchique.
Tip: A sight-seeing tour through Monchique is recommended.

Everybody vies for the summit! But even a walk in the valleys of the Monchique hills exudes a certain charm. Without a great deal of effort, you

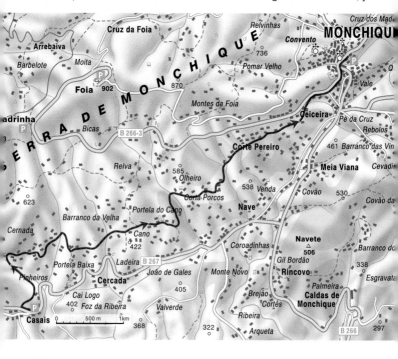

can experience a diverse natural sylvan landscape with gorges, hamlets and expansive views. Unfortunately, in the summer of 2003 and 2004, forest fires ravaged the Monchique hills so that our route may have been impaired. Across from the bus stop in **Casais**, a gently ascending forestry road begins by heading north through cork oak and deciduous forests and after 600 m passes by the farmstead of Pinheiros. Bearing right, continue along the trail for another kilometre until reaching a junction. Here, turn right onto a trail leading in a broad bend swinging to the right that becomes a path and after 400 m leads to the scattered houses of **Portela Baixa**. Pass by numerous other properties and then after 250 m reach a fork in the trail; bear left here.

Now continue for another 500 m without much of an ascent until reaching the next junction; here bear left again. After a short stretch of trail, passing cork oaks, turn right along an ascending trail. At the next fork bear left again then pass by the Casa Cristobal; behind the house, bear left to swing soon onto a path leading to a narrow dirt road. Following this, pass through **Cano**. At the next fork, turn left and ascend for 1 km to reach the houses at **Corta Porcos**.

Now swing right for the last time onto our final trail that brings us after a good 1 km to the houses of Olheiro. After crossing through a small valley, arrive at **Corte Pereiro**. Another 2 km later, the trail merges with the road that leads to Fóia but we descend right along this to reach the village limits and then continue bearing left to end up at **Monchique** centre where the bus station is located.

Monchique and Fóia.

29 From Monchique to the Fóia, 902 m

Panoramic trail on the highest summit of the Algarve

Monchique – Fóia-summit

Starting point: Monchique, 420 m. Final stop for the bus line Portimão – Monchique. By car: from Portimão along the N 124 and N 266, from Aljezur along the N 267. Parking possible at the main square or at the large car park located somewhat further to the north.
Destination: Fóia-summit, 902 m. Only accessible by car (signposted starting at the main square in Monchique); large car park.
Walking times: Monchique – Fóia-sum-

mit, 1½ hr (6.6 km).
Ascent: 500 m ascent.
Grade: Because of the ascent, strenuous walk along trails, paths and a narrow tarmac road.
Einkehr: Restaurants and bars in Monchique and on the Fóia.
Tips: Before beginning the walk, we recommend a leisurely sight-seeing tour in Monchique. Caldas de Monchique, a thermal spa located 6 km south, is also worth a visit.

Beginning in the quaint mountain town of Monchique with its pretty squares, unique shops, a manuelin-style church and the ruins of the cloister Senhora do Desterro, this walk continues through cork oak and pine forests.
It is best undertaken during stable, clear and beautiful weather because the main attraction is the sweeping view from the Fóia summit over the entire western Algarve.

Bird's-eye view of Monchique.

Start at the central square Largo 5 de Outobro (bus stop). With our backs to the street that we used to arrive here, cross over the square and turn right onto the Ria de Porto Fundo then immediately bear left onto the stepped street Travessa the Guerreiras. Now follow the signs and ascend to the **cloister Senhora do Desterro**.
In front of the ruins of the Colegio de Santa Catarina turn left, then at the following fork bear right. Ignore the next two small streets turning off to the right and continue climbing along a sweeping left-hand bend which opens a lovely bird's-eye view of Monchique. Reach the cloister complex which was damaged during the great earthquake

in 1755 and has since fallen into rack and ruin (plans have been made to turn this into a luxury accommodation!).

At the cloister, turn right to ascend through a cork oak wood. After 200 m turn left onto an old trail ascending steeply for 400 m to reach a narrow tarmac road. Take a short turn left along this only to turn immediately right along the continuation of our trail and after 200 m turn left onto a path. In the shade of a forest, ascend for another 300 m passing by a trail merging from the left. 400 m further on, another trail merges from the right. It is only a few metres more of steep descent to reach a narrow tarmac road; turn right. Continue ascending along the tarmac and ignore all merges and forks that follow. At first enjoy the shade of the forest and then – with our goal appearing before us – continue the steep ascent along numerous switchbacks. Soon the narrow road leads through pastureland and abandoned terraces. Beyond a last bend in the road – at first to the right, then to the left ascending past the car park – arrive at the panoramic summit. The cluster of antennae and radar equipment spoils things a little, nevertheless, the view remains electrifying, stretching from the west coast over the densely populated south and all the way to the hilly countryside to the west with its treasure trove of walking trails. A completely different attraction can be found in the souvenir shops next to the restaurants. Nowhere else in the entire Algarve have we found such a selection of keepsakes and curiosities as are on offer here. Take your pick if you like! The return route retraces the approach route or drive back from here by car or taxi (no bus connections available). Possibly you can arrange a trip back with one of the many excursion busses.

Additional circular routes in the Serra de Monchique can be found in the map »Trilhos de Bio-Park Network« which can be purchased in Monchique. Whoever wishes to escape the summer heat and the noisy beach areas for a few quiet days of walking in the cooler mountain landscapes, will find in Monchique, and even more so, in the newly restored spa Caldas de Monchique, unique accommodation with historic charm.

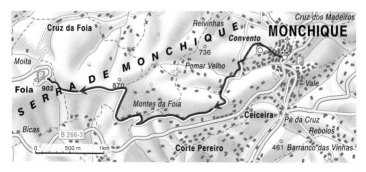

30 Circling the Fóia

Panoramic circular route on the highest peak of the Algarve, the Fóia

Fóia road – Madrinha (803 m) – Pé do Frio – Chilrão – Fóia road

Starting point and destination: Car park on the Fóia road, 750 m. Only accessible by car. From Monchique (main square) follow the signs for »Fóia«. Car park 6 km on (200 m past an overlook in a sharp right-hand bend).

Walking times: Car park – Madrinha ½ hr, Madrinha – Pé do Frio 1 hr, Pé do Frio – Chilrão ½ hr, Chilrão – car park 1½ hr; to-

tal time 3½ hr (13.5 km).

Ascent: 460 m of ascents and descents.

Grade: Due to the difference in altitude and steep descents, this walk is somewhat strenuous, leading along woodland and field trails as well as little-used roads.

Refreshments: Restaurants on Fóia's summit and along the mountain road are available but not during the walk.

Especially the sweeping views of almost the entire western Algarve make this walk so appealing.

In order to locate the somewhat overgrown trailhead, we start by standing in the car park with our backs to the street. From the top of a metres-high ramp, we spot a path in front of us and follow this to the left. Walk parallel to a slope until a forest fire lookout tower appears to the right (perched on the Madrinha, our first goal). Here the path swings right. Descend slightly through *macchia* then through a eucalyptus wood. At the first fork, bear right, at the second fork shortly after, bear left. The path swings out of the woods to the left skirting around a natural depression then to the right ascending slightly.

Pass through more eucalyptus. Still bearing right and ascending, after 1.5 km meet up with a dirt road. Climb along this to the right and then 500 m on at a fork, once again bear right and ascend steeply to the summit of the

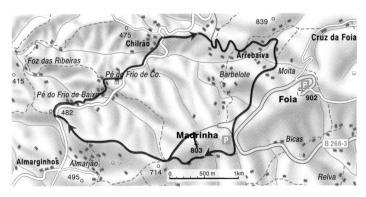

Our walking realm at the foot of Madrinha.

Fóia foothill **Madrinha**. Retrace your steps along the approach trail and after 1.5 km return to the merge. Continue along the dirt road that descends steeply through a dense wood for 2.5 km; below the summit, meet up with a tarmac road.

Since the old trail still exists, cross over the road and turn immediately right along this trail which keeps parallel to the road and heads towards the hamlet of Pé do Frio de Baixo. After a good 100 m arrive at a fork and once again bear right. Another good 100 m further on, take the grassy path straight on and pass under some fruit trees. This soon descends slightly into a long left-hand bend and then heads directly to the village centre of **Pé do Frio**. Here ascend right to the tarmac road above and then turn left; continue along this for the next 2 km until reaching the hamlet of **Chilrão**.

A street forks left towards the houses and a few metres later, a dirt trail merges from the left into the tarmac road; ignore both of these. Afterwards – directly before the road takes a sharp right-hand bend – turn right onto a broad dirt trail. Always remain on this broadest trail steadily ascending in long, drawn-out zigzags. 2.5 km after leaving the tarmac road behind, do not continue on the descending trail heading straight on, turn left instead. A good 100 m on, turn left again and after another 600 m along the dirt trail, bear sharply right and 100 m further on again to the left. The trail swings in a long bend to skirt around a valley and then finally heads straight towards the summit of Madrinha. Shortly before reaching the car park, bear left at a fork in the trail to continue the ascent and conquer the last metres while taking in lovely views.

31 Picota, 774 m

Along shady trails to the Fóia's neighbouring summit

Monchique – Picota summit – Monchique

Starting point and destination: Monchique, 420 m. See Walk 29 for the approach route.
Walking times: Monchique – Picota summit 2 hr, Picota summit – Monchique 1¼ hr; total time 3¼ hr (11.2 km).
Ascent: 420 m of ascents and descents.

Grade: Due to the sometimes steep ascents and descents, this is a somewhat strenuous walk along trails, paths and little-used tarmac roads.
Refreshments: Restaurants and bars only in Monchique but not at all during the walk.

This is a nicely-shaded walk for hot, sunny days along well-marked trails passing through forests.

Begin the walk in **Monchique** by the bus station. After 400 m of walking and passing the large car park on the N 266 (signposted for Lissabon) turn diagonally to the right descending to the district of Cruz dos Madeiros. 150 m on, at the village limits, turn right onto a narrow tarmac road that soon becomes a trail. After 400 m, bear right onto a path that crosses over a trail and meets up with a broad trail at the valley floor.

Follow this to the left until merging into a narrow tarmac road. To the right and descending, cross over the little river and immediately after, turn left. This trail crosses over a stream and continues, passing a house on our

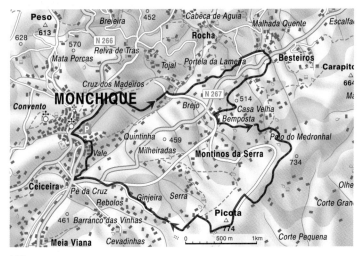

left-hand side, as a grassy trail. At the next fork, turn right onto a path that ascends steeply between walls. The path broadens into a road and then merges into a narrow tarmac road; turn left here to continue the ascent. After 700 m along the tarmac and before reaching a place where cork bark is collected (to our left) and in front of a house on the right, turn onto a path that opens up lovely views. After a few metres of crossing over fields, once again enter a dense wood. Bearing steadily left, ascend steeply to the **Monchique – Alferce road** (N 267).

Take this road left and after 50 m turn right onto a broad trail. Quickly reaching a fork, do not bear left to ascend, instead bear right along the broad trail that traverses parallel to the slope and passes a house after 150 m. 300 m through dense forest reach a couple of buildings, behind which a view opens up to Monchique and to Fóia

50 m on, the trail merges into a narrow tarmac road that we follow to the left (to the right, we can spot the tarmac road onto which we will soon be merging). In front of a farmstead surrounded by plantations, turn right onto a grassy trail and after 200 m of ascent turn right onto a road that leads to a broad tarmac road.

Ascend left along the road for only a little less than 100 m then turn left onto a path passing through the eucalyptus wood before meeting a tarmac trail after 300 m; turn left onto this trail. At the forks 500 and 600 m on, bear to the right both times. Pass by plantations then through a farmstead after 500 m. 200 m later, past a left-hand bend, continue straight ahead at a fork. When 800 m further on, a trail merges diagonally from the right, we have to pay close attention to the next fork (directly on the other side of a pass). Here, the arrows point to a broad trail to the right which continues for 600 m, towards the end as a woodland path and eventually meets up with a tarmac road. Follow this to the left until it ends; here a clearly marked rocky path begins our push to the **summit**.

On the opposite, south-westernmost side of the peak, dot trail markings guide us over granite rock to the beginning of a trail, however this is not our return trail. Instead take the woodland trail that immediately forks off to the right and descends steeply for 2 km. Now continue the descent to the left along a road, pass the next merge 800 m on to the right and finally, after having passed a number of farmsteads, turn left onto the Monchique – Alferce road.

If you wish to avoid walking the last metres along this busy main road, turn sharply right when meeting the N 266 ascending from Portimão and walk back in the direction from which we came, descending to a farmstead. Here, an ascending trail leads to the left and heads for the village. Bear right when crossing over a trail, then swing left along a narrow road that swings again to the left to return to the main road. Here, turn right to finally reach the bus stop and the parking place.

In the Hinterland of the Barlavento

None of the »hinterland walking regions« is easier to reach than the hilly landscape between Silves and Salir where these eleven walks are designed to lure you. Each tour embraces a separate natural area – from the river wetlands around Silves through to the panoramic hills near Alte. Each walk also includes a visit to one of the historic cities or to one of the picturesque villages. None of the other regions offers the visitor a simpler gateway to the Algarve's Moorish heritage as does this walking region.

Should one give the most praise to Silves, the capital city of the Algarve during the century-long rule of the Moor? Or does Alte have a better claim to the throne with its quaint historic centre and its springs? But you cannot forget Salir that forges all of these qualities into a compact space. Lastly, not only a few walkers claim that the tours around the Castelo Paderne are the most beautiful to be found in all of the Algarve. Obviously, there is no other choice than to lace up your own walking shoes to seek out your personal favourites among these most beautiful of Algarve routes. When you find yourself captivated by this region, accommodation is available in Silves, Alte and Loulé.

Cork collection point at Salir.

Enchanting flowers in Salir.

32 On the Rio Arade

From Silves through fertile farmland to a bird sanctuary

Silves – Encherim – Arade-Levada – Rio Arade – Ilha do Rosário – restaurant »Mira Rio«

Starting point: Silves, 35 m. Bus service to Lagos and Albufeira. Railway station 2 km away. By car: from Portimão along the N 124 or from the motorway exit Armação de Pêra along the N 269 (well signposted). Parking possible on the ring road along the Rio Arade.

Destination: Day-tripper's restaurant »Mira Rio«, 25 m. Bus service to Lagos. By car: along the N 124 Silves – Portimão, 4.2 km past Silves. Large car park at the restaurant.

Walking times: Silves – Encherim ½ hr., Encherim – Arade-Levada 1 hr, Arade-Levada – Rio Arade 1¼ hr, Rio Arade – Ilha do Rosário ¼ hr, Ilha do Rosário – restaurant »Mira Rio« ½ hr; total time 3½ hr (15.4 km).

Ascent: 150 m of ascents and 160 m of descents.

Grade: Despite a steep ascent, an easy walk along paths, trails and tarmac roads.

Refreshments: Only at the starting point,

the destination and at the café on the Rio Arade.

Alternatives: 1. You can cut the walk short by turning left at the second crossing of the *levada* then continuing on for 600 m returning to the approach road. Turn right and retrace your steps along the road until reaching Silves's centre (¾ hr). 2. The walk on the Ilha do Rosário is also possible to make as a circular walk. Beginning at the restaurant »Mira Rio«, 1½ km on, turn left onto a narrow tarmac road after having crossed over it twice before then immediately turn right to ascend along a track and pass through the hamlet Vale de Lama. Always keep to the broadest track and do not turn left after 600 m. Not quite 2 km on, the track merges into the walking route described below.

Tip: The historic centre of Silves with a Castelo and episcopal church is worth a visit.

Rio Arade – once a lifeline, now quietude itself.

Silves, the Algarve's capital during the Moorish era, is known to all. No one should let their holidays in the Algarve end without visiting this lovely town with its former episcopal church Sé and, above all, the ancient *Castelo*. As to the manifold natural treasures offered by the richly diverse landscapes, these can only be captured by a walk which extends the city sightseeing ramble to an adventurous excursion. Remember to bring your binoculars along for some bird-watching!

Begin the walk in **Silves** at the central square Praça do Municipio with the city hall and the Torreão das Portas de Cidade. Pass through the archway of the gate, once a part of the city's fortifications, to ascend left to the Sé church (behind the church and to the right, the way to the *Castelo* can be found).

Directly in front of the cathedral, turn right and then 50 m on, turn diagonally left onto the Rua do Castelo. In honour of the name, this street descends beneath the castle walls for 400 m. Turn left at the first crossing and turn right

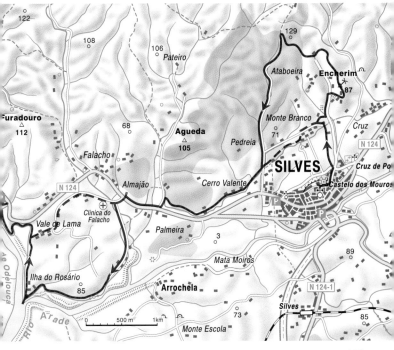

immediately after onto a trail keeping to the right of an orange grove and heading north. After 200 m, the trail swings slightly right then left and keeps parallel to an abandoned trail flanked by walls. 300 m on, another right to left swing is made. By the **house »Vivenda dos Chaminés«**, we reach the *levada* for the first time; during the rest of the walk, we will meet up with this watercourse time and again.

Turn right and follow the *levada*, with the watercourse running at our left-hand side. At the beginning of an aqueduct, a path descending right leads to a road; turn left onto the road only to immediately fork off twice bearing right both times. Head towards the hillock **Encherim**, capped by the ruins of a windmill.

After 300 m, turn right onto a narrow tarmac road; 50 m on, turn left. In front of a house, swing right; now immediately turn left to climb up to the overlook. Silves lies before us, with its battlement-crowned castle – towering in the distance, the »hotel-crowned« skyline of Portimão. To the left, the view sweeps over extensive farmland giving way to the chain of hills marking the Serra do Caldeirão; behind us lie the heights of the Serra de Monchique and right, the wetlands of the Arade River through which we will soon walk.

With your back to the castle, continue along the ridge trail. After 800 m, pass alongside a fence where goats usually graze on the other side then turn left and descend to a junction. Here and at another junction 150 m on, bear right. In a sparse eucalyptus wood reach a fork after 200 m and turn sharply left. Another 150 m on, climb up to the right and then descend. 500 m further on, turn sharply left and head south. Now begin a descent. Ignore the first left fork after 700 m but take another 700 m later – bear left onto a track

that becomes a tarmac road. 200 m on, turn left and then turn right along steps and ascend to a tarmac road to follow this left for 150 m until a trail to the right climbs up to reach the *levada* once again.

Here, turn right (following the 1st Alternative route, turn left) and follow the *levada* along the watercourse path. Cross over a narrow tarmac road after 300 m. Another 250 m later, the *levada* draws near to the N 124 and follows this road for 1 km.

After a long swing right, when the *levada* passes under the road and converts again to an aqueduct, turn right along the road for another 300 m until a track forks left (sign »Club Nautico«). Turn left here and left again after 200 m (from the right, the trail from the 2nd Alternative merges).

Cross through a fertile valley for almost 1 km. After completing the crossing, first pass underneath the *levada* then climb up to it once again. After 500 m, the *levada* is gathered up into a conduit. Now ascend right, following blue and red trail markings then descend again to Silves' »river of fate«, the **Rio Arade** 250 m further on.

A café awaits us to the left, with canoe rentals and a taxi boat that can bring us back to Silves, another alternative, but we only cast a passing glance in that direction. Instead, we continue following the *levada* and after 1 km reach the confluence of the Ribeira de Odelouca with the Rio Arade. When we go off to the left onto the promontory, the **Ilha do Rosário** lies directly across from where we stand: a first-rate spot for a break.

Now the time has come to unpack our binoculars because the following kilometres offer fantastic opportunities for bird-watching. On the other side of the river, wetlands draw storks, herons and other wetland birds also nesting here.

After 1 km, a narrow tarmac road merges from the right at a water pumping station. Approaching from the opposite direction, the 2nd Alternative route forks off left at this point. 300 m on, cross over the narrow road once again. Continue left again along the *levada* which winds through luxuriant citrus groves and finally, after another kilometre, to the **restaurant »Mira Rio«**. In front of the restaurant, steps ascend to the right to reach the large car park.

A quiet companion – the levada from Silves.

33 To Castelo Paderne

Circular walk along the Ribeira de Quarteira to a Moorish *castelo* near the medieval »Via do Infante«

Boliqueime – Castelo Paderne – Boliqueime

Starting point and destination: Boliqueime, 70 m. Bus service to Albufeira and Faro. Railway station on the Faro – Lagos line. By car: signposted from the motorway IP 1 (exit 2) and from the N 125. At the village limits, turn left towards the cemetery and park along the access road.
Walking times: Boliqueime – Castelo 2¼ hr, Castelo – Boliqueime 2 hr; total time 4¼ hr (23.4 km).

Ascent: 240 m of ascents and descents.
Grade: Due to stretches without a path in the dry stream bed, a more difficult walk along paths, trails and a narrow tarmac road.
Refreshments: Only available in Boliqueime.
Alternative: From the *Castelo*, you can combine the route described in Walk 34 to reach Paderne in ½ hr (bus station).

Many walkers consider this route along a river bed to be the prettiest of all in the Algarve's hinterland. What spaced-out societal drop-outs once searched for in Quarteira is free for the taking in the heavenly natural landscape along the river flowing there: pleasure for pleasure's sake.
A level path passes through lush, teeming flora accompanied by the twitter of birds, otherwise, absolute tranquillity, old mills, a bridge from the Roman era, a Moorish castle ... for anyone whose senses have not been hopelessly deadened, rich nurture can be found here.

At the southern village limits of **Boliqueime**, on the minor road leading to the centre, a narrow road turns left and ascends steeply to the cemetery (signposted). Our walk begins here. Keep straight ahead on the narrow tarmac road, ignore the turn-off to the cemetery then descend along the dirt road to the valley of the **Ribeira de Quarteira**.
1.2 km past the starting point, in front of a farmstead on the left, turn right onto a country lane. Take the lane 250 m up the river until reaching an easy crossing for the little river. The amount of water flowing here varies a lot depending on the season.

On the other side, pick up a path and turn right upstream. Red dots mark the path which keeps to the valley floor; therefore ignore all ascending forks to the left or right! The path follows the course of the river in wide bends crossing through groves of fruit trees and past olive and carob.

After not quite 4 km along this relaxing fluvial ramble, the valley opens up and the many fascinating ruins of watermills draw the walker to a break and a look round.

When during the route ahead, the valley begins to narrow, the path switches from one side and then soon to the other side of the now dry river bed. Another 250 m further on, the path continues for 400 m along the stony river bed itself.

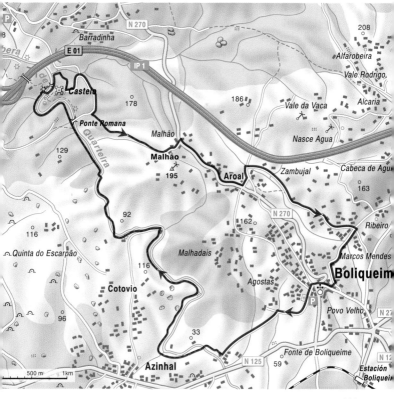

Now ascend once again – in the direction of our walk – to the river's right bank, only to switch soon after again to the left bank for the last 1.5 km.

Finally, arrive at the **Roman bridge**, over which the route connecting Sagres to Andalusia has passed for thousand of years. Far above the harmonious arches of the bridge and in the background, tower the brick walls of a Moorish castle – the **Castelo Paderne**. Do not climb directly to the castle, instead continue on for almost another 1 km passing under trees and through Spanish cane along the river's left bank – in relation to the direction of our walk – until reaching a renovated mill (Azenhal) which is worth a visit. Depending on the water level, ford the river in front of the mill or cross over a bridge past the mill. Shortly before reaching the motorway overpass and an access road to the right ascending to the *Castelo*, turn right onto a footpath that climbs steeply and considerably shortens our storming of the castle.

The tree-spotted square in front of the castle or the panoramic inner courtyard (although without shade) are ideal spots for a leisurely break. In 1249, the Moor was ousted from this bastion, one of the last on European soil. The little 15th- century church proves that the complex was used even during the Christian era. Exactly when was the fortress – today appearing so small in comparison to the motorway running directly next to it – abandoned once and for all?

To return, take the narrow dirt road that leads diagonally to the left from the square in front of the castle. After 150 m this meets up with another path;

Fresh flowers in ancient ruins.

Moorish castle of Castelo de Paderne.

turn right. 250 m on, when the path leads in a long, right-hand bend down to the river bed, turn left onto a country lane that ascends quickly and steeply. After 1 km of climbing, ignore a steep-sided trail to the right then meet up with a junction where we continue along the path straight ahead. Drystone walls line the path to the left and after 500 m meet up with the Paderne – Boliqueime main road; turn right.

750 m on, pass a store on the left-hand side of the road with a peculiar post box. Directly past the store, turn left onto a country lane. Ignore the two trails turning right and take the first broad ascending trail left that crosses over a hillock and then descends into a little valley replete with fields and groves of fruit trees. Here turn right onto a dirt trail descending down the valley.

More and more villas appear between the gardens. After climbing up this dusty road for 2.5 km, meet up with a junction of a tarmac road. Turn right and descend the last kilometre until reaching the village limits of **Boliqueime**.

Here continue descending and bearing right to reach the village centre with bar/restaurants and a bus stop. Descend further along the main road for another 200 m to come to the turn-off for the cemetery – a reminder to celebrate your vitality after such a lively tour!

34 Along the Via do Infante do Sagres

A walk along an old connecting trail, charged with history

Paderne – Castelo Paderne – Amoreira – Azenhal – Paderne

Starting point and destination: Paderne, 70 m. Last station for the bus from Albufeira. By car: via the motorway IP 1 then along the N 395. From there, signposted for Paderne. Parking possible at the village limits or turn right (signposted »Castelo«) and after 1½ km at the Fonte de Paderne.
Walking times: Paderne – Castelo ¾ hr, Castelo – Armoreira 1 hr, Armoreira – Paderne 1½ hr; total time 3¼ hr

(14.5 km).
Ascent: 210 m of ascents and descents.
Grade: Easy walk along trails, paths and narrow tarmac roads; a steep descent from the *Castelo*.
Refreshments: Bars in Paderne and Armoreira, plenty of water at the Fonte de Paderne
Tip: The 16th-century church in Paderne with manuelin-style ornamentation is worth a visit.

The starting point for our »travel through time« is **Paderne**'s centre. Perhaps you should pay a little »warm-up« visit to the little Muralha church displaying Gothic and Moorish elements. Climb down the street towards Purgatório but turn off onto the second street to the left (signposted »Castelo«). After a good 1 km reach the sprawling complex near the Fonte de Paderne. The road swings left here but instead follow the narrow dirt road that forks right. Through plantations of orange, quince and olive trees, head towards the motorway overpass that at first hides the view of the castle. Cross under the overpass then at the fork following just after, bear right and then immediately left onto a path that climbs up to the *Castelo*.

Don Alfonso III took the castle in the year 1249; the little Gothic chapel was built on in the 15th century. Today, only some old clay brick walls bear witness to the splendour and undaunted sturdiness of this fortress in days long past. Our gaze drops down to the valley of the Ribeira de Quarteira; for thousands of years, the Roman bridge (renovated in the 16th century) served a section of the ancient connecting road that later fell under the protection of the Moorish castle. Standing in front of the castle with your back to it, turn right onto a path that at first leads alongside and to the left of the castle walls. At the end, swing left and zigzag down to the valley floor. Here, turn left along a distinct path through the dense vegetation. A good 1 km beyond the castle, we find ourselves standing in front of the bridge that is said to have survived since the Roman era.

Cross the bridge, turn left and after a few metres turn right onto an ascending path. After a climb that puts us in a bit of a sweat, we reach a terraced plot. The wall on the other end marks the spot where a trail continues on; turn left along this trail. Follow the trail to swing right and after merging into an intersecting trail, go left. Pass by a hut of corrugated iron on the right and head for the motorway overpass. 100 m beyond the bridge, ignore the right-hand turn onto a dirt road and instead continue along the trail flanked by walls and heading straight on. The trail reaches a narrow tarmac road and then swings right towards the houses of **Amoreira**. For the route ahead, turn right here onto the narrow tarmac road that at the end of the village turns right and descends along numerous bends passing beneath the motorway. The next motorway is crossed by bearing left and then right and finally over a bridge. Afterwards, turn left and pass beneath the sign »Azenhal« (= mill) then descend. At the valley floor, swing right to reach the renovated buildings of an old mill. Follow the valley trail for 1 km through dense thickets of reeds and lush vegetation until returning to the Roman bridge. Once again, cross over the bridge. This time, however, turn right and follow the trail which immediately swings left ascending a slope and opening lovely views. At a trail merging from the right after 300 m (Walk 33 forks off here), turn left and pass by the castle hill again, before beginning a descent on the other side along the approach route and passing under the motorway. Cross over flourishing fields; soon reach the spring and finally Paderne's centre.

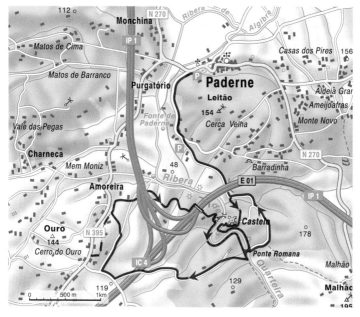

35 In the Barrocal

Panoramic circular route through the green oasis near Alte

Santa Margarida – Cerro – Pico Alto (276 m) – Cerro – Santa Margarida

Starting point and destination: Santa Margarida, 230 m. By car: from the N 124 at the village limits from Alte; turn left twice to head for Santa Margarida (a good 2 km from Alte). Parking possible in the village centre.

Walking times: Santa Margarida – Cerro ½ hr, Cerro – Pico Alto 1½ hr, Pico Alto – Cerro 1¼ hr, Cerro – Santa Margarida ½ hr; total time 3¾ hr (17.4 km).

Ascent: 350 m of ascents and descents.

Grade: Easy, although due to a steep ascent, a somewhat strenuous walk along trails, paths and little-used roads.

Refreshments: Bar/restaurants only in

Alte. En route, you could take a 25 min detour to the restaurant in Azinhalinho.

Tips: Along the approach or, better still, along the return route you really should pay a visit to the Fonte Santa. To get there: not quite 1 km past Santa Margarida bear to the right onto a narrow road and after 300 m reach the spring on the right-hand side. The waters of the spring are reported to possess healing powers.

Also, if you have yet to visit Alte, you must allow yourself to be treated to the service offered in this »white village«, just as lovely as it is hospitable.

Why is it so beautiful in the Barrocal? This area is a geological oddity! A limestone reef stretches from Cabo de São Vicente in the west to a spot north of Tavira, supporting an extraordinary spectrum of flora. Many species of orchids only bloom in this region and farmers have also found fertile soil here. This plot of God's earth is distinguished through groves of fruit

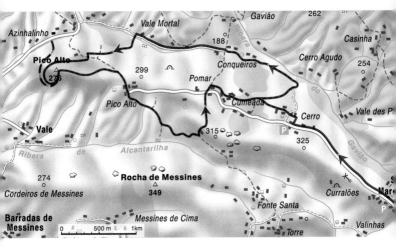

Ascent to Pico Alto.

and almond trees (in January and February beautifully blooming in different shades of white and pink) as well as rich, cultivated fields lying between bustling hamlets. For these reasons, especially in the springtime and in the autumn, the Barrocal is a pleasant place to go walking.

In the village centre of **Santa Margarida** follow the sign »Cerro« to pick up the little-used, panoramic narrow tarmac road heading northwest. The fertile hills of the Barrocal lie before us and further to the north, the woodland countryside of the Serra de Caldeirão. After a good 2 km reach the village limits of **Cerro**.

Turn right and cross through the farming village along a narrow cobbled road. At the other end of the village, cross over a track coming from the left and then continue past the last houses of the hamlet. When the trail ends after 200 m, turn right onto a path that swings left a few metres further on at the very last house.

Unfortunately, the old cobblestone trail is sometimes overgrown so that we must at first cut to the right and then 250 m later, to the left along paths. 1 km past Cerro meet up with a fork. Bear left to reach the first houses of **Cumeada**. Here we meet up with our return route but now turn sharply right along a steeply descending country lane. After 350 m, reach a narrow dirt road descending from Cerro; turn left heading down the valley. 1 km on, at first descending and then climbing up, pass by the picturesque **hamlet Conqueiros**. Here continue the ascent and ignore a number of forks that ascend to the right to farmsteads.

Not until 2 km past Conqueiros, when meeting a track to the right that ascends to a large farmstead with stables and silos, turn off left along a path just past a gigantic cork oak. Continue past a fieldworker's shed on the left then pass an intersecting trail to continue straight ahead along a country lane while still climbing with the hillock ridge of the Pico Alto in sight. Pass left of a fence supported by concrete posts then continue past a stream. Above a water reservoir, 400 m after leaving the lane behind, turn right onto a path. Cross over an old watercourse and an intersecting trail then head towards a ruin, passing by this on your right to continue through an almond plantation and ascending left. After not quite 1 km, the path leads to a trail; turn right.

Enjoy the sweeping views while traversing the slope and descend slightly along a wide bend to the left. Below us, to the right, we can make out the houses of Azinhalinho. A car park usually filled with cars at the southern end of the hamlet marks the location of a highly-recommended restaurant. After a total of 600 m along this trail, we reach a junction. If you would like to take a break, descend right to reach the restaurant (10 min descent, 15 min ascent). The main trail climbs up to the left and – a somewhat strenuous stretch with gravel underfoot – finally swings left to reach the panoramic summit of **Pico Alto**. It's true that this summit is only 276 m above sea level but due to its exposed position, the peak opens up an extraordinary view reaching far away to the Monchique hills.

From the summit, head back again for 50 m and turn left through a break in the wall. Immediately after, turn right onto a path that leads along the hillock ridge towards the east. After 400 m, ignore the first trail forking right and head towards a tall tree to pass this to the left. Climb up to a rise that opens up a backwards view including Pico Alto and continue another 500 m along the hillock ridge. Soon, a number of wall-enclosed trails lead to the right and to the **hamlet of Pico Alto**. Once there, turn left to reach a narrow track at the village limits. Turn right onto the track only to leave it again after a few metres by turning left onto an old, descending field path.

Ignore the first trail forking right at a water reservoir and also ignore a trail merging from the right. Not until 500 m past the village do we turn right onto a descending country lane that we leave behind again by bearing left onto a path at the fork 70 m on. 200 m later, reach another country lane; turn left and ascend steeply. Cross over the track coming from the direction of Pico Alto. Now turn right onto a path that runs parallel and after 200 m reach the first houses of the **hamlet Cumeada**. Since the village trail cannot be used, turn left passing between the houses and at the village limits beneath a tall carob tree, turn right to ascend until meeting a path coming from the hamlet where we turn left.

Surprisingly enough, after 150 m, we reach some renovated houses and pass along the front side of these to the right and then in a swing left. Our path has now become a track; when the track swings right, fork off left onto a path that passes to the right of a tumbledown house and at the same time meets up with the merge described earlier. Now retrace our steps along the approach route to return to Cerro and further on to **Santa Margarida**.

The sweeping view from Pico Alto.

36 Rocha dos Soidos, 467 m

From Alte to the exposed panoramic mountain Rocha dos Soidos

Alte – summit of the Rocha dos Soidos (467 m) – Alte

Starting point and destination: Alte, 200 m. Accessible by bus from São Bartolomeu. By car: from the N 124 in Alte at the eastern village limits, follow the signs for »Fontes / Fonte Grande«. Parking possible there.

Walking times: Alte – Rocha dos Soidos 1¾ hr, Rocha dos Soidos – Alte 1¾ hr; total time 3½ hr (11.8 km).

Ascent: 320 m.

Grade: Due to the difference in altitude, a somewhat strenuous walk along trails, paths and little-used tarmac roads.

Refreshments: Only available in Alte

Alternative: In the sharp left-hand bend before the ascent, continue straight ahead along the country lane in a swing to the left and then to the right to reach a country inn after 1 km.

Tip: The churches, the springs, the shops and the bar/restaurants in Alte are worth a visit.

Follow the narrow tarmac road that leads to the Fonte Grande further up the valley. The road becomes a broad trail then 700 m past the **Fonte Grande** forks left onto a path flanked by walls. When the path sometimes becomes indistinct while passing through newly-planted olive groves, follow it the best that you can and ascend in a wide bend to the left. After 750 m, meet up

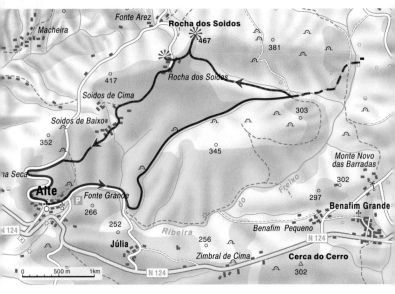

with a broader path and turn diagonally to the right. 100 m on, ignore a path forking left and continue the same way along a small valley and ascending. Even when the path forks and finally becomes a narrow dirt road which at first descends easily and then more steeply, maintain the direction and continue up the valley.

We have walked almost 5 km since the Fonte Grande. Across from where we stand and on the other side of the narrow tarmac road, the prominent peak of the Rocha da Pena rises up (Walk 38). Here, in a hair-pin bend, turn sharply left onto a trail that leads alongside a fence and gradually but steadily ascends. After 1.2 km along this trail, bear right at a fork and then swing right

View from Rocha dos Soidos.

after 150 m, now climbing even steeper. Our path passes twice through fence gates. At the next fork, ignore the country lane forking left (on the return route, this will bring us to the village Rocha dos Soidos) and bear right passing a concrete building. Continue 250 m along an ascending path crossing the limestone rock until reaching a surveyor's point marking the **summit of the Rocha dos Soidos** (467 m). Perched on a steep outcrop, this is a lookout par excellence!

The return route retraces the approach route until reaching the first junction of the ascending path. Here, turn right along a country lane that in 200 m brings us to the village limits of **Rocha dos Soidos**. Cross over the tarmac road that bends to the right then immediately afterwards pick up a path that leads over fields to the right to reach a viewpoint that offers a superb backwards view of the summit.

Return to the road, turn right and pass through the village. At the western village limits, turn left onto a path that descends steeply. Soon this becomes a trail and after 1 km reaches the first houses of the hamlet **Soidos de Baixo**. At first bear right and then left to pass through the hamlet and meet up with a tarmac road; turn right here. Along many bends with many lovely views, the road leads for the last 2.5 km towards **Alte**. At the village limits, swing onto a narrow street to the left that leads to the village centre. Here, next to the church, bar/restaurants await, as well as signs that point left to the **car park at the Fonte Grande**.

37 Circling Alte

A panoramic circular walk over the foothills of the Rocha dos Soidos

Alte – plateau on the foothill (340 m) – valley of the Ribeira de Alte – Alte

Startingpoint and destination: Alte, 200 m. Bus connection from São Bartolomeu. By car: from the N 124 in Alte at the eastern village limits, follow the signs for »Fontes / Fonte Grande«. Parking available there.
Walking times: Alte – foothill summit 1¼ hr, foothill summit – »fertile valley« ½ hr, »fertile valley« – Alte 1¼ hr; total time 3 hr (12.3 km).
Ascent: 200 m.
Grade: Due to the differences in altitude, a somewhat strenuous walk along trails and paths.
Refreshments: Only available in the town of Alte.

For those who just want to take a day's excursion from the Algarve coast to the heavenly hinterland, we highly recommend the »white village« of Alte with its famous Fontes (springs), noteworthy church, artist colony and hospitable taverns. The route described here includes the outskirts of the town and the luxuriant vegetation found along pleasant walking trails.

The narrow tarmac road that led us to the Fonte Grande sets the direction for the walk. The road becomes a broad country lane following the course of a wide stream up the valley for 2 km. Ignore all trails turning off right or left – our broad trail is correct.

Shortly before the trail crosses the stream, turn left along a country lane that quickly ascends through *phrygana* vegetation to a citrus fruit plantation. After 800 m ascent and when a trail merges from the left, continue the climb, heading straight on and passing through a large orange plantation. At the **top**, enjoy a sweeping view stretching from the Rocha dos Soidos to the north (Walk 36) and over to the southern coast not far away.

From this detour, we retrace our steps back to the trail and then turn left. The trail descends in a long left-hand bend to skirt around the slopes of the foot-hill. To the right, the summit of the Rocha da Pena looks down upon us (see Walk 38).

After not quite 2 km, the valley widens and we reach a wet, fertile and inten-sively-farmed plain at the edge of which, in autumn, a rich harvest of grapes, pomegranates, almonds and a cornucopia of other fruits await us. Bear to the left and walk along a country lane continuing along the valley floor for a good 2 km and heading back again.

1.6 km on, a path merges from the right onto the trail which has become narrower. After a long right-hand bend meet up with the approach route. Now it is only a few strides to the right to reach the **car park at the Fonte Grande**.

Fertile valleys near Alte.

38 Nature reserve Rocha da Pena

To the panoramic Rocha da Pena with extraordinary vegetation

Rocha – the summit of Rocha da Pena (479 m) – Penina – Rocha

Starting point: Rocha, 325 m. By car: from the N 124 in Taipa (about 1 km west of Salir) follow the signs for the Rocha da Pena. Parking possible at the Fonte dos Amoados in Rocha's village centre.
Walking times: Rocha – summit of Rocha da Pena 1 hr, summit – Penina ½ hr, Penina – Rocha ¾ hr; total time 2¼ hr

(7.8 km).
Ascent: 200 m.
Grade: Strenuous walk along trails and paths. The descent to Penina is a rocky one.
Refreshments: Cafés and bars in Rocha and Penina.
Tip: The Nature Reserve Centre in Pena.

This panoramic walk leads through the extremely interesting limestone region of the Barrocal. The nature reserve zone of the mountain ridge Rocha da Pena (»mountain of condolence« or »mountain of punishment«) presents the walker with a unique spectrum of flora including rock roses, heather and lavender. The peak is enveloped by sprawling expanses of *matos* and is an ideal nesting place for owls and buzzards.

Begin at the square in **Rocha**'s centre. The beautifully ornate Fonte dos Amoados (»fountain of love«) offers a dreamy place for a short break. The »good water of the mountains« is cherished by the inhabitants because it is reported to be effective in relieving certain health problems.

The way to the peak begins to the left of the café; a sign points the way to Rocha da Pena. The 2 km long summit chain offers us an impressive view to enjoy already during the first few metres of our steep ascent. To the south, a view opens up of the Picavessa hills lying on the opposite side. The broad dirt trail turns right after 250 m and leads east in a gradual ascent below the cliff face of the Rocha.

After not quite half an hour, reach a clearing with a carob tree as a centrepiece. Well-marked with coloured dots, the ascending summit trail swings west here and continues as a path along the left edge of the ridge.

The best view of the Caldeirão hills to the north and including Monte Malhao's peak can be enjoyed by taking a 200 m long detour straight ahead northwards.

Not quite 1 km further on, the trail to the summit crosses a stone wall built during the Neolithic period and continues past another such stone wall. After 500 m, cross a man-made clearing and then begin a descent. Just before this descending trail, take the marked path to the left ascending through scrub to reach the summit of **Rocha da Pena**, topped by a surveyor's point.

From the summit, retrace the route along the path for a few metres to return to the ascending trail and continue along this by turning left and westwards. A steep path that descends directly to Penina from here should not be used – a foolhardy short cut. Also, the marked trail that crosses over yet another ancient stone wall and then continues in a wide bend left and finally ends up in Penina is really steep and stony as well as dangerously slippery with scree underfoot. The trail merging from the left offers a much better surface for the final descent to **Penina**.

Trail markings lead us through this typical village, at first left to a small square graced by a fountain. Afterwards, turn into the third street to the right. This leads to a café. Along the intersecting street into which we soon turn left, exit the village by walking east.

Directly past the village limits, fork left onto a track. A little later turn right onto a footpath at a junction of three trails. This leads alongside a farm building and through fields. 400 m beyond the village, when the path meets up with a track that approaches from the right, follow this without changing direction and keep parallel to the summit chain of the Rocha da Pena, always to the north of the Penina – Pena road, until reaching **Rocha's centre**.

Rocha de Pena – rugged but easy to climb.

39 The windmills of Rocha

Short circular walk in the Barrocal

Rocha – windmills – Rocha

Starting point and destination: Rocha, 325 m. By car: from the N 124 in Taipa (about 1 km west of Salir) follow the signs for the Rocha da Pena. Parking possible at the Fonte dos Amoados in Rocha's village centre.

Walking times: Rocha – windmills 1 hr, windmills – Rocha ¾ hr; total time 1¾ hr (6.2 km).

Ascent: 200 of ascents and descents.

Grade: Moderately strenuous walk along dirt trails and sometimes steep and rocky paths.

Refreshments: Bar/restaurant in Rocha.

Tip: The Nature Reserve Centre in the village of Pena located on the other side of the valley provides information concerning the distinctive characteristics of the flora and fauna found in the Rocha da Pena Nature Reserve.

In days gone by, how fruitful must have been this limestone-rich, hilly countryside of the Barrocal! Numerous windmills bear witness to the past glories of this »granary of the nation«. Nowadays, and especially in springtime, the flowering splendour of the environmentally-protected slopes of the Rocha da Pena bring joy to all and sundry; here, we pick up the course of our walk.

After an invigorating draught from the »spring of love« (Fonte dos Amoados) at the square in **Rocha**'s centre we begin our walk along the marked dirt trail signposted »Rocha da Pena« which begins steeply ascending to the left of the bar/restaurant. After 250 m, turn right and begin a gradual climb under the cliff walls of the Rocha da Pena. Another 750 m on, we reach a clearing with a remarkable carob tree. At this point, Walk 38 continues to the left and on to the summit.

We continue straight ahead on the country lane and after 250 m fork off right onto a path that crosses over the brow of a small hillock. Now a steeper and

stonier descent follows until a path merges from the right. Continue in the same direction towards the windmill and take a swing to the left around the edge of the hillock. After 750 m, our path merges onto a track. Turn right here and 200 m on, bear left for the last 250 m until reaching the **windmills**. A marvellous spot to take a break and take in the views!

With no alternative, our route ahead retraces the 300 m back to the last junction. We have to make a decision here: either to return to the clearing with the carob tree and then follow Walk 38 to ascend to the summit or – the shorter version – to fork off left here and onto a trail that aims for the little village of Pena on the other side of the valley.

We choose the second, cross over a panoramic hillock ridge and descend 800 m to the tarmac road while passing between two reservoirs. Swing to the right and climb up through the lovely valley for the last 1.2 km until reaching the houses of **Rocha**.

Beyond the Barrocal – the Serra do Calderão beckons.

40 Circling Salir

A circular route through richly diverse farmland

Salir – Rio Seco – Salir

Starting point and destination: Salir, 270 m. By car: approach via the N 124 or take the IP 1 (exit 3) then take secondary roads as signposted. In Salir, there is a car park in front of the health centre.
Walking times: Salir – Ribeiro Seco 1 hr, Ribeiro Seco – Salir 1½ hr; total time 2½ hr (11.6 km).

Ascent: 130 m of ascents and descents.
Grade: Easy route along country tracks and paths.
Refreshments: Bar/restaurants only available in Salir.
Tip: Salir's church, the houses of the picturesque village and the ruins of a Moorish fortress are worth visiting.

From the car park in front of the health centre, take the street towards Loulé and climb down the valley of the **Ribeira dos Moinhos**. After not quite a kilometre, turn left in front of the bridge spanning the river onto a country lane. 300 m further on, skirt around to the left of a farmhouse along a path. After another 300 m, the path turns right in front of a farmstead and shortly afterwards swings left to meet up with a broader path. Turn right and follow this 100 m to a tarmac road; here turn right onto the road and begin an ascent.

400 m further on, turn left in front of a farmstead onto a country lane signposted »Fujanca« and immediately afterwards turn right onto another trail. 200 m later, a broad dusty road merges from the right; bear left onto this and begin a descent. 800 m further on, ignore a trail forking right that leads to a farmstead. Directly afterwards, follow another trail to the right which leads along a wall. 200 m on, meet up with a fork to continue straight ahead.

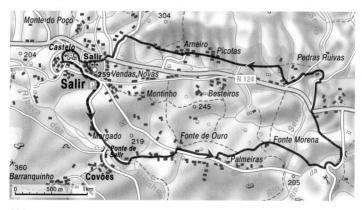

The Moorish town of Salir.

Cross over the **Rio Seco** 150 m later. Crossing the **Ribeira da Salgada** shortly after proves to be somewhat more difficult; head right and upstream to locate the stepping stones for the ford. After crossing the river, bear right and then in a left-hand bend ascend to a narrow tarmac road. Climbing down to the left brings us back to the river. Directly past a bridge, turn left onto a country lane. 500 m on and after a stream bed crossing, swing right to meet up with the N 124 and cross over it. A country lane brings us in 250 m to another crossing of the Rio Seco. After crossing, bear left 250 m to reach a broad trail that approaches from the road; turn right onto this trail and ascend. Passing cork oaks, head towards a little house and turn left in front of it. After not quite 2 km, the trail reaches the hamlet **Arneiro**.

At the village limits, take a short cut by heading straight on to ascend along a steep, concrete-paved trail which meets up with a country lane after a few metres. When this lane soon takes a swing left, continue straight ahead along a path that becomes another country lane then a narrow concrete road. Turn left 1 km past Arneiro and head for the N 124. Follow this for a short stretch to the right until reaching the turn-off of a narrow road; turn onto this and ascend to the town. To reach the pretty church, climb up to the left. For a visit to the ruins of the Moorish fortress, take the narrow road from the church descending straight ahead then ascend and swing onto the first street that ascends to the right. In front of the bar/restaurant, ascend to the right to finally reach the ruins of the fortress where lovely views can be enjoyed. To return to the car park, go back to the bar/restaurant and descend along the narrow street; turn left onto the main street and at the crossing, turn right onto the street heading towards Loulé.

41 In the hilly countryside of Monte Seco

A classic mountain and valley walk – worlds away from the Algarve coast

Ribeira de Algibre – Monte Seco (296 m) – Charneca – Ribeira de Algibre

Starting point and destination: Ribeira de Algibre, 100 m. By car: from the IP 1 (exit 2) towards Loulé. After 2 km, turn left towards Parragil. From there, turn left towards Benafim Grande. 4 km on, in Ribeira de Algibre, parking possible in front of the bridge spanning the river.

Walking times: Ribeira de Algibre – Monte Seco ¾ hr, Monte Seco – Charneca ½ hr, Charneca – Ribeira de Algibre 1½ hr; total time 2¾ hr (10.6 km).

Ascent: 350 m of ascents and descents.

Grade: Easy walk along country lanes, only somewhat strenuous due to steep ascents and descents. After rainfall, some slippery stretches!

Refreshments: Bar/restaurant in Monte Seco (The owner speaks French well).

Alternative: After descending into the valley of the Ribeira de Algibre, you can turn left to continue as far as you wish along country lanes leading along the level valley and passing through lovely cultivated gardens. Return along the same route or connect up with another scenic walk along a narrow dusty road that leads north to Espargal or south to Parragil.

Tip: Loulé, the historic monuments, the pilgrimage church and the morning market are all worth seeing.

Along the road that was used to drive here, a country lane forks left before the bridge spanning the Ribeira de Algibre. After 50 m, turn right onto another country lane that keeps parallel to the river. Follow this for 1 km until reaching a fork. Here, bear left along the steeply ascending trail. In the **hamlet Monte Seco** meet up with a tarmac road and turn diagonally right. Immediately after, turn right again to continue along a country lane that is at first tarmac and leads out of the village. Ignore the first fork left 100 m on and not until reaching the second, after another 400 m, turn left to begin an ascent.

Village tableau in Monte Seco.

Now climb steeply left for 1 km. After crossing over the crest of the pass, the trail swings into a right-hand bend. Here, fork left onto a country lane heading towards a farmstead. In front of the farmstead, ascend cross-country to the left and over stone walls to finally reach the **summit of Monte Seco**.

Now return to the ascent route and continue along this to reach the renovated houses of **Charneca**. De-

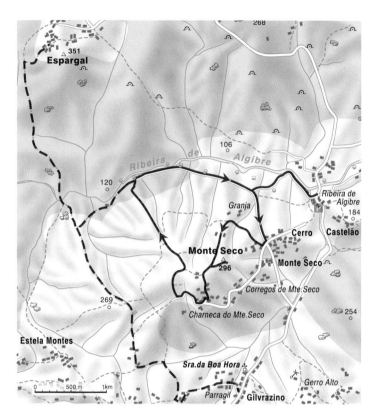

scend left to the tarmac road. Follow the tarmac road for 250 m ascending right and continue by bearing right along what is now a country lane. At the first fork in the trail 100 m on, bear right again. After 150 m, pass to the left of a house and at the next two forks always bear left following the descending rocky trail. Aim steadily towards the valley.

At a high voltage pylon after another 600 m long descent, ignore a fork right and continue along our trail swinging right and reaching the valley floor. Here, swing right onto the valley trail (left if following the Alternative walk to Espargal or Parragil).

Following the valley, retrace the approach route along the familiar narrow country road to return to the little village of **Ribeira de Algibre**.

42 In the nature reserve »Fontes de Benémola«

A ramble to caves and springs, to picnic places and old farmsteads surrounded by almost tropical vegetation

Car park »Fontes« – caves – basket-maker – car park

Starting point and destination: Signboard for the nature reserve 270 m. From the N 396, turn left 9 km north of Loulé along the N 524 towards Tor; after 3 km (300 m before the bridge crossing the stream) park at the signboard.

Querença has bus service to Loulé; the walk could also begin there (see map).

Walking times: Car park – springs – caves – car park 1½ hr (6.5 km); from Querença 3 hr (12.5 km).

Ascent: 50 m of ascents and descents, Alternative 150 m.

Grade: Easy ramble along marked trails and paths with only one short steep ascent.

Refreshments: Only available in Querença.

Alternative: If you want to begin the walk in Querença, start at the lofty, panoramic village square with its pretty chapel. Take

the steeply descending narrow street 300 m down to the little-used N 524 and turn left onto this. At a street junction 600 m on, continue straight ahead as signposted. After another 1.7 km, a narrow dusty road which is signposted and marked forks off to the right to join the walk described below.

On the return, you can retrace along the same narrow road, or you can fork off after 1.2 km onto the track to the right that merges onto a narrow tarmac road not quite 2 km on. Follow this to the right for 1.5 km through a lovely lush and flowering landscape until reaching the crossing described below where we turn left to return to Querença.

Tips: The parish church of Querença with lovely views, the Grotto of Salustreira and the sacred Rocks of Assumada da Cruz are worth a visit.

This is a short ramble full of surprises. The flora along the Ribeira dos Moinhos changes from cork oak woods to cultivated plots of olive, fig and carob groves, to thickets of scrubland with walnut trees and reaches the climax at the springs with an almost tropical tangle of Spanish cane and oleander. On top of all this, caves can be discovered and explored – be sure to bring along a torch! Finally, you can visit the workshop of a basket-maker.

At the information signboard »Fontes de Benémola« take the gravel trail here to the right until

reaching a fork after 1200 m. (The return route for the Alternative walk forks right.) Fork left and on the other side of a shallow valley 800 m on, reach the first of the springs that has lured us for a long time with its bubbling; descend left to the spring along steps leading through dense thickets of cane. A few metres further and to the left, a wooden bridge crosses over the **Ribeira dos Moinhos** (the bridge was unfortunately broken at the time) where we can pick up our return route.

Until the bridge is repaired, stepping stones above the next spring serve to ford the stream. To continue to the caves, we must forge further on and straight ahead.

At a small dammed-up pool, a picnic place has been established under a gigantic carob tree. Here, a steep and narrow path forks right to ascend to the caves. You can also reach the caves in a long bend to the right by continuing along the trail that leads straight ahead along the stream. Both caves narrow very quickly so that you can only penetrate to a depth of about 15 m. Perhaps around 7000 BC, the first inhabitants of the Algarve actually dwelled here in this fertile region?

For the return route, we retrace our steps to the bridge or to the stepping stones above the dammed-up pool. Now cross over the stream to the right and bear left following the signs; reach a farmstead after 800 m. A basket-maker willingly demonstrates his handiwork based on ancient tradition.

After our visit, continue for another 1.2 km parallel to the stream until meeting up with the N 524. Take this to the left and over the bridge then turn left again and climb up the last 500 m stretch to reach the car park.

A watery walk.

In the hinterland of the Sotavento

This is a vast walking region, stretching from the hills around São Brás de Alportel through historic Estói, the panoramic Cabeça and to the river wetlands of the mellow, green Rio Guadiana which acts as the border to Spain. Fortunately all of the starting points for these walks are easy to reach from the western Algarve thanks to the little-used motorway IP 1. These are destinations well worth the trip since the eastern Algarve offers a completely different set of lovely attractions than those found to the west.

Awaiting our visit are the cork oak forests around São Brás de Alportel, excavation sites from the Roman era and the romantic palace gardens at Estói. Waterfalls can be discovered here, gushing year-round in liquid plenitude that puts to shame the notion of an Algarve lacking in fresh water. Another densely forested nature reserve area awaits us in the countryside around Tavira, as well as villages nestled and hidden »over the hills and far away«. Presenting a completely different picture is the scenery around the river border: salt flats and vineyards, barren hills and fertile plains; the easternmost walk in the Algarve is also well worth taking and leads us to new highlights. Lodging can be found in Santa Bárbara de Nexe, São Brás de Alportel, Estói, near Moncarapacho (Quinta da Fortuna), in Santa Catarina da Fonte do Bispo (12.5 km north-west of Tavira), in Vila Real de Santo António and in Alcoutim on the Rio Guadiana.

In the palace gardens of Estói.

Lush vegetation on the Rio Guardiana.

43 In the countryside of São Brás de Alportel

Near-tropical forests lead to Fonte Ferrea

Fonte Ferrea – overlook – merge of the EN 2 – Fonte Ferrea

Starting point and destination: Fonte Ferrea, 287 m. By car: from the N 2 near the village of Alportel, turn off at the signpost »Fonte Ferrea«. Park at the picnic grounds 300 m on.
Walking times: Fonte Ferrea – overlook ¼ hr, overlook – the merge of the N 2 ½ hr, the merge of the N 2 – Fonte Ferrea ¼ hr; total time 1 hr (4.4 km).
Ascent: 200 m of ascents and descents.
Grade: Due to the steep ascent, a short

but strenuous walk along paths, trails and narrow tarmac roads.
Refreshments: Only the spring offers water for refreshment.
Alternative: From the picnic place at the spring, numerous trails and paths lead through the bordering woodland. There are many possible combinations to make by connecting these rambles and walks of varying lengths or by hooking them up with the described tour.

The Algarve offers new surprises time and again. Who could imagine that a mere 20 km from the coast and only a few kilometres beyond the densely populated basin at São Brás, an almost tropical jungle of woods exists? In springtime, this walk presents a bouquet of colourful flowers and throughout the year offers shade galore and refreshing relaxation at the fount, usually only bustling with visitors at the weekend. Even on weekends and public holidays, only a few metres into the woods and walkers can find solitude again.

Begin the walk at the **Fonte Ferrea** and cross over the Ribeira do Alportel along the suspension bridge to the bank opposite the spring. Take a trail for 200 m; to our left, the stream bubbles and murmurs. When the trail turns left, bear right along an ascending trail. A meadow lies to our left. After 400 m a steep path begins, climbing diago-

nally left. Finally, the path ascends out of the woods to reach fields spotted with trees and to an overlook with a view sweeping over the wooded valleys.

A good 1 km is behind us now as we meet a broad intersecting trail; turn right here. The trail begins as a panoramic ridge trail and then descends. After 500 m the trail returns to the forested valley of the Ribeira do Alportel. After crossing the river, swing left and after 200 m, right. Now tarmac, the trail ascends to the

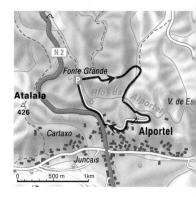

N 2 and reaches this 450 m further on. After turning right along the N 2, only a short stretch follows before reaching the turn-off. Now finish up with a pleasant descent along the narrow tarmac road to end up at the fortifying, iron-rich waters of the spring.

In the »jungle at the Fonte Ferrea«.

44 In the Serra do Caldeirão

Through the hills to the north of »the cork capital« São Brás de Alportel

São Brás de Alportel – Tareja – Vale de Estacas – São Brás

Starting point and destination: São Brás de Alportel, 260 m. Direct bus connections to Faro. By car: along the N 2 to São Brás. Parking possible near the central square Largo de Sao Sebastiao (intersection of the N 2 and the N 270).
Walking times: Largo de São Sebastião – Tareja ¾ hr, Tareja – Vale de Estacas ¾ hr, Vale de Estacas – Largo de Sao Sebastiao 1 hr; total time 2½ hr (11.2 km).
Ascent: 300 m of ascents and descents.
Grade: Moderately strenuous walk along trails, tarmac roads and paths which are

often rocky.
Refreshments: Only available in São Brás.
Alternative: Especially on hot days, you should avoid the second steep ascent by continuing along a valley trail starting at the tumbledown mill (kilometre 3.6). After 500 metres of level walking, at kilometre 5.2, this trail merges with the route described below.
Tip: The church, the bishop's palace and the Museo Etnografico do Trajo Algarvio in São Brás.

Begin the walk at the Largo de São Sebastião and take the Avenida de Liberdade to the right. After 200 m, turn left onto the broad, four-lane main road (signposted »Sanatorio«). 700 m on, at a minor roundabout, turn right and immediately afterwards left onto an overgrown trail that climbs upwards. The trail crosses tarmac roads after 150 and 300 m then soon becomes tarmac itself as it begins a descent and then swings to the right. Another 300 m on, finally reach a road junction and a Moorish well.

Here turn sharply left along an ascending narrow tarmac road. After 250 m, a trail forks off to the right but we take the next road to the right 50 m later on the other side of the hilltop. At first the road is tarmac and leads past villas then continues in a descent as a trail flanked by walls to reach another tarmac road 300 m later.

Turn right along this road. Turn left onto another wall-enclosed trail 100 m further on. At a fork after 200 m, bear left in a descent to meet, 300 m on, yet another narrow tarmac road; turn right here. Not quite 100 m later, turn left then ascend alongside of a wash-house and, another 100 m on, turn left to reach the centre of the hamlet **Tareja**.

Only a few metres later, the narrow street swings right and becomes a path climbing up to a little plateau. Continue along the path which occasionally broadens only to narrow once again and steadily descends through sparse copses of delightful cork oaks. Ignore two trails forking off to the left.

After having descended for 1 km, meet up with a track merging from the right and follow this by turning left. Ignore the trail forking off to the right 50 m later as well as the trail forking off to the left 100 m on. After another 400 m, reach a fording spot at the **Ribeira de Alportel**.

By high water, turn left upstream for 15 m to cross over stepping stones. 100 m on and after a swing to the left, the steepest stretch of our route begins behind a tumbledown mill. Already described as an Alternative walk, you can avoid this ascent by continuing straight ahead along the valley trail. The prettier choice is to take the country lane to ascend to the right, following alongside and to the right of a pond and climbing up to a line of fence posts. After 600 m, the lane merges onto a ridge trail with lovely views; continue the ascent along this trail by turning left.

400 m later, fork off to the left at a junction and begin a steep downhill climb. Our next destination – the hamlet of **Vale de Estacas** – appears far below us. Our trail passes a newly built villa to our left; at a fork, bear right. After 600 m, reach the little river once again. The Alternative route merges here from the left.

Cross over the course of the river and turn right onto a path that leads along the riverbank. Once in the village, turn left. Reach the tarmac road after 300 m. Follow this to the left for 400 m until reaching a little transformer station. From the crash barrier here, pick up a path to the left descending to the stream.

After crossing the stream, begin an ascent alongside it. Pass through a dense wood to the left of and alongside a riding stable. The path becomes a trail then reaches a narrow road leading past houses to meet up with a tarmac road 700 m on; turn diagonally right onto this road. After a few metres, turn off to the right and cross over the valley floor, passing gigantic cork oaks to finally reach the little village of **Tesoureiro**. After 400 m and after another 100 m, turn left both times. Follow the main road for 400 m until reaching a junction. Turn right and ascend for 600 m to return to the familiar approach route.

Continue ascending straight ahead and then descend, bearing right at the well. Finally turn left onto the overgrown path and return along this for 850 m to the wide road. After another 700 m, reach the main square in **São Brás** where restaurants (and our vehicle) await.

45 Guilhim, 313 m

Through verdant gardens and groves of fruit trees to a panoramic peak

Estói – Milreu – Guilhim summit – Lagos e Relva – Fialho – Estói

Starting point and destination: Estói, 100 m. Bus connections to Faro. By car: signposted from the IP 1 (exit 5). Parking possible along the streets leading to the village centre.

Walking times: Estói – Milreu ¼ hr, Milreu – Guilhim summit 1 hr, Guilhim summit – Lagos e Relva 1 hr, Lagos e Relva – Fialho ½ hr, Fialho – Estói 1 hr; total time 3¾ hr (16.5 km).

Ascent: 380 m of ascents and descents.

Grade: Strenuous walk due to steep ascents and descents along country trails.

Refreshments: Bar/restaurants in Estói and in Lagos e Relva.

Alternative: The walk can be cut short as follows: from Guilhim's summit, descend back along the approach route for 200 m

then turn left onto a country lane that reaches a narrow tarmac road after 400 m. Take this to the right for 1 km to return to the approach route a good 300 m from the bridge crossing over the motorway (here bear left).

Tips: A visit to the gardens of the 18th-century palace of the Viscondes de Estói (open from 10 a.m.–12:30 p.m. and 2 p.m. –5 p.m., closed Sundays and Mondays). At the archaeological excavations at Milreu, the ruins of a country home from the Roman era display rare and impressive mosaics (opening times as above; closed Mondays). In the visitor information centre, an educational computer animation presents all of the Algarve's historic points of interest.

This is a walk for art lovers and history buffs just as much as for connoisseurs of beautiful natural scenery. Very few tours can offer such a wealth of noteworthy historic monuments in such a small area. In addition, we pay a visit to a viewpoint high above Faro and the wetlands of the Ria Formosa – and stroll past architecturally unique modern country homes.

In Estói, return on foot to the excavation site of Milreu along the main road that we drove in on.

From the exhibition zone, continue to the right along the road for a few paces and then cross over the **Rio Seco**. Continue straight ahead over the (watch out!) busy intersection and then turn right onto a country lane beginning here. The lane becomes a tarmac trail and after 600 m turns right to cross the bridge over the motorway. Passing houses, continue 100 m to reach a fork; swing left here. After another 200 m, at a well, turn right onto an ascending path. 300 m on, reach a narrow tarmac road (here the return route of the Alternative walk merges from the right). Turn left and immediately after, turn right onto a narrow dusty road that passes by the **hamlet Guilhim**.

Now begin the push to the summit. Cross over a trail 300 m on, continuing straight ahead in the same direction along a path that narrows until it ends after another 300 m. Now pick up the traces of paths that lead steeply upward and to the right along terraced plots; these are easiest to cross if you

Grace in the park of Estói.

follow along the left-hand edge. Soon the main path broadens and after a
300 m long climb reaches a trail that has ascended from the right (this is the
descent route for the Alternative walk).

Continue the steep ascent along the broadest path even when another trail
merges from the right 100 m further on. A little wall must be negotiated and
then we have reached the mountain ridge. Through dense *phrygana* vege-

tation continue left to reach the obelisk – the highest and most panoramic point (313 m above sea level) of the **Guilhim**. Particularly impressive is the view of Faro and its surroundings.

After a leisurely break on the summit, turn right – with your back to the ocean – and climb down along the steep, rocky trail. 500 m on, a trail merges from the right. Continue another 500 m along the mountain ridge. When the trail swings left towards a farmstead, turn off sharply right to descend to a crossing of tarmac roads; continue straight ahead here and ascend. When the narrow road starts to descend after 400 m, turn right to climb down to another narrow road that leads left to reach the centre of **Lagos e Relva**. To the right and past the bridge, you can find a bar/restaurant that is recommended.

The route ahead begins here by turning sharply left onto the tarmac road that leads towards Bordeira. After 150 m, turn diagonally right along a narrow road that ascends steeply and soon becomes a country lane. The lane leads at first along the right side of the ridge, changes to the left side, then back again, but in any case it continues north for a good 1 km. Pass by the ruins of a number of windmills. Now turn right onto a narrow tarmac road and after 200 m, turn right onto an old cobblestone trail passing alongside a house. After another 200 m, turn left along a trail that becomes a path flanked by drystone walls. Pass the villas lying to the right and use the concrete car tracks that steeply descend in 300 m to a stream bed. Turn right

Roman ruins in Milreu.

here, continuing the descent to reach a tarmac road in the valley of the Rio Seco (bus stop!).

Cross over the street and the little river as well; maintain the same direction when meeting a fork to the left and after 100 m, pick up the lower trail that quickly ascends leading along parallel to the river bed. Not quite 1 km on, continue straight ahead and do the same after another 500 m when a trail forks off to the left. Not until another 100 m further on, turn left along a narrow dusty road that passes a home for the elderly. Cross over the motorway and at the junction immediately afterwards, continue straight ahead on the dusty road to reach the town of **Estói**. Pass under a little bridge to cross between the palace and the gardens. If you want to pay a visit to the palace gardens, turn right before reaching the first square and then immediately right again along descending steps and a path that lead directly to the entrance of the gardens and to the bizarre palace.

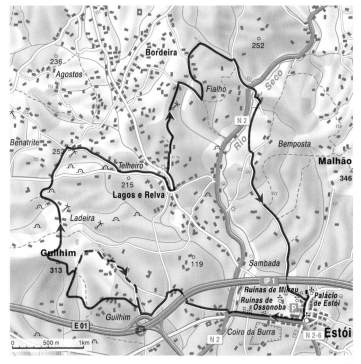

46 Cerro da Cabeça, 249 m

Panoramic trails through cultivated garden landscapes

Car park at Cabeça – Cerro da Cabeça summit (249 m) – car park

Starting point and destination: Car park at Cabeça, 80 m. Bus service to Moncarapacho. By car: along the IP 1 (exit 6) and the N 398 to Moncarapacho. At the village limits, first head towards Fuseta then Luz and finally towards Cerro da Cabeça, each time turning left. After 2 km, park when the tarmac ends.
Walking times: Car park – Cerro da Cabeça summit 1¼ hr, Cerro da Cabeça summit – car park ¾ hr; total time 2 hr (7.2 km).
Ascent: 190 m of ascents and descents.
Grade: More difficult due to the differences in altitude and rocky trails.
Refreshments: In Moncarapacho. Nothing available en route.
Tips: The parish church in Moncarapacho; the panoramic peak of São Miguel (410 m), accessible by car.

Due to a lack of shade, we recommend taking this impressive walk between October and May. The route leads along the grey limestone hump of the panoramic mountain Cerro da Cabeça high above the cultivated flowering farmland of the Sotavento.
Begin the walk at the gate entrance to the left of the road between two white concrete posts. The trail straight ahead through the gate is not private; we can use it. Head right and pass the »Casa da Misericordia«. At the fork after 150 m, bear right onto the gravel trail lined by telegraph poles. Another 250 m further on, pass the ruins of a small industrial complex to our left where the line of poles comes to an end.

Along the ascent ahead follow the yellow slash trail markings that will change to green and white dots on the summit plateau. After a total of 1.3 km, the gravel trail (sometimes paved) turns off sharply left. Some 100 m in front of us is a villa. Two huge fire rings about 10 m in diameter, 900 m beyond the bend and to the right of our route, are old limekilns. Now the trail climbs steeper and becomes a path at the end, leading through thick undergrowth on the rise. After another 400 m, reach the south-western

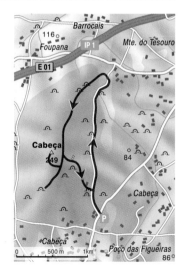

outcropping of the **Cabeça reef** to enjoy a view of the coast and of the Sotavento countryside as well as the dome of São Miguel. The column marking the reef summit is somewhat troublesome to reach along paths through dense, thorny *matos*; at the end, even a bit of scrambling is required. The 360° view is a just reward for this short stretch of exertion.

For the push to the final peak, return 400 m along the ascent path until a broad path noticeably marked with green dots, forks left. This ascends through thick underbrush that sometimes almost completely hides the course of the path. Three rock barriers are easily negotiated by some scrambling using handholds. After ascending for 400 m, reach the concrete column at 249 m above sea level. A virtual all-embracing »bird's-eye view« is here at the **Cerro da Cabeça**.

After enjoying the breathtaking views, we must set forth on our return route. Scramble the 400 m back to the merging of our approach route and retrace this path to the left for 200 m. A broad path, also marked with yellow slashes, turns right to reach the ruins of a house with an observation tower that had already caught our eye at the beginning of the walk. Reach this after 400 m. Lo and behold, a stepped trail awaits us for the final descent. 700 m of pleasant, leisurely and panoramic descent – what a crowning touch to this summit foray! At the ruins of the industrial complex, the path merges back onto our approach trail. Another 400 m right and return to the parking place.

The rugged Cerro da Cabeça.

47 To the Moinhos da Rocha waterfall

Through the watery realm of the Rio Sequa springs

Car park on the Rio Sequa – Moinhos da Rocha waterfall – car park

Starting point and destination: Car park in the valley of the Rio Sequa, 15 m. Bus and rail connections only in Tavira. By car: from the IP 1 (exit 7) along the N 270 towards Tavira then along the N 125 towards Vila Real. After 500 m, turn right towards Tavira. Before the river, turn left along the narrow road leading along the riverbank. After 5 km, turn right towards »Cachopo«. Park immediately after the turn-off.

Walking times: Car park – waterfall 1½ hr, waterfall – car park 1 hr; total time 2½ hr (10.3 km).

Ascent: 100 m of ascents and descents.

Grade: Easy walk along paths, country trails and little-used narrow tarmac roads.

Refreshments: Nothing available en route. Restaurants and accommodation available in Tavira.

Alternative: If you only wish to visit the waterfall and the springs of the Moinhos da Rocha, drive past the car park mentioned above and continue along the tarmac road for another 3.5 km then turn right to cross over the little river. From the end of the tarmac road, it is only another 100 m along a dusty road to reach the car park »Pego do Inferno« (»the throat of hell«) and a 500 m walk to descend to the beautifully designed picnic area. Walk along a broad country lane then turn right and over steps to reach this area.

Tip: The wealthy, classicist town of Tavira, just as historic as it is picturesque, is well worth a visit.

Due to a lack of shade, this walk is highly recommended in springtime and in autumn. For children, this is the perfect exciting alternative to the complaint »nothing but swimming, nothing but sandy beaches«.

Cross the Rio Sequa over the concrete bridge without railings. Pass a farmhouse and meet up with the N 397. Turn left towards Cachopo. After 200 m, past a bridge and in a right-hand bend, turn left onto a narrow dirt road. Now the route leads parallel to the river for a long time and passes through a fertile landscape teeming with groves of citrus trees and stands of bamboo. After 2 km the road forks directly in front of a little river tumbling down from the

The Cascata Moinhos da Rocha.

right. Here, bear right to descend to the Rio Sequa and cross over stepping stones. On the other side of the river, walk a few paces left and then turn right following a path climbing up a little embankment. Cross through fields and 100 m on, meet up with a dirt trail near a farmstead. Turn left and follow this trail for not quite 2 km until reaching a fork and steps descending to a picnic area and continuing down to the waterfall. We have finally reached our goal and can savour a lovely view of the **Cascata Moinhos da Rocha** that even in summer freely flows and tumbles down into an emerald lake. At the weekend, this fresh water paradise is a favourite excursion for the townspeople of Tavira.

After an invigorating dip and a leisurely rest in these lovely surroundings, the route back returns to the steps and ascends to the dirt trail. 500 m left, reach the car park for the Alternative walk. We continue straight ahead for 100 m then turn left onto the narrow tarmac road to the bridge spanning the **Ribeira da Asseca**.

At the crossing, bear left. Another 3.5 km of walking awaits us, heading down the valley along the tarmac (little-used on workdays) and passing through groves of orange trees and under carob and medlar trees to reach the car park.

If you prefer not to visit the town of Tavira (which is well worth seeing) you can drive from the car park along the narrow road to the left of the river bed – relative to the direction being driven – and head toward the waterfall. At the junction after 3.5 km, keep left to reach the N 270. Turn left along this road and soon you will come to the entrance ramp of the motorway (Tavira exit).

Through the Mata Nacional, a unique state-owned forest

Car park Mata Nacional – Malhada do Peres – Daroeira – Asseiceira summit (108 m) – car park

Starting point and destination: Car park at the Mata Nacional, 68 m. By car: from the N 125 Faro – Vila Real, 3 km past the bridge spanning the Rio Gilão near Tavira. Turn left 300 m past the turn-off to the Eurotel (signposted »Almargem« and »Pension«). After 700 m, turn right and cross over a little bridge and immediately after, turn left. 800 m further on and again another 900 m after that, turn left both times. Beyond Solteiras, cross under the motorway and reach the large car park (forester's house above and to the left).

Walking times: Car park – Malhada do Peres ¾ hr, Malhada – Daroeira ¼ hr, Daroeira – Asseiceira summit ½ hr, summit – car park ½ hr; total time 2 hr (8,9 km).

Ascent: 230 m of ascents and descents.

Grade: Easy circular route along broad forestry trails and little-used tarmac roads. The alternative walk is more difficult due to steep descents along paths.

On this walk, beyond a belt of sparse eucalyptus woods and lush river wetlands, we find pretty little villages where time has stood still. Especially in springtime, we can enjoy lovely views while passing through a colourful sea of flowers that blanket the fields and wrap around groves of trees. In summer, only the wooded sections offer a little shade.

We start at the car park with our backs to the motorway. Follow the tarmac road to the north-east for 200 m then turn left (sign for Malhada do Peres). After 50 m,

Refreshments: Nothing available en route.

Alternative: After the ascent to the Asseiceira, 100 m further on when the plated trail turns right, turn left. Now a steep cross-country descent follows the traces of a path to reach the valley floor. Along a washed-out ravine from the valley floor ascend diagonally right until reaching a rocky trail near two carob trees. Turn onto the trail then continue for 300 m. Now descend slightly left to reach a saddle. Along a path here, climb down towards a field and then, in front of the field, turn right to the river. Cross over a bend in the river along stepping stones. On the other side, pick up a narrow forestry road climbing left up to the tarmac road.

when the tarmac road takes a right-hand bend, fork off left. Remain on the broad forestry road passing through eucalyptus woods.

The trail forks after 1 km. Fork off to the right and reach a fording place after 200 m. On the other bank, bear left onto the broader, ascending dirt road. After 700 m ignore a broad trail forking off left and after another 200 m reach the most surprising highlight of the tour: the crest of a pass that suddenly opens up a superb view of the intensively cultivated hilly farmland. Between lush and colourful fields, the white villages seem almost to be hovering. To our left lies **Malhada do Peres**. Descend straight ahead to the edge of the village.

After 700 m, a sign points the way to the right towards Daroeira. Follow along the course of the Ribeira da Zambujosa to cross this after 600 m. At the fork immediately following, bear right. 300 m after and below the village, bear right again. Descend 300 m later to the little river and cross over this once more. The steep ascent which follows will be completed 300 m on. Here meet up with a narrow dirt road approaching from the right; follow this to the left. Continue on for another 900 m and join a narrow tarmac road to the right in between villas. 400 m on, a cobblestone trail lures us to the right to ascend to the panoramic summit of the **Asseiceira**. For the final »push to the peak«, fork off left onto a path 20 m before a villa.

If you prefer not to take the Alternative route during the descent, return back to the tarmac road. To the right descend once again to the Ribeira da Gafa and cross the river over a bridge 500 m later. Now return to the woods of the state-owned forest. After 800 m, the broad trail of the Alternative route merges from the right. 100 m further, bear right for 400 m to reach the starting point of the walk. Finally reach the car park after another 200 m.

Lovely villages in the pastoral countryside.

49 Reserva Natural do Sapal de Castro Marim

Circular route through a nature reserve

Car park – salt processing plant – pumping station – car park

Starting point and destination: Car park at the entrance to the nature reserve, 10 m. Bus and rail connections to Vila Real de Santo António; bus service in Castro Marim. By car: from Vila Real de Santo António along the N 122 towards Castro Marim. After 1.6 km, turn left onto a narrow dusty road and 200 m on, park to the left of a tumbledown building.

Walking times: Car park – salt processing plant 1 hr, salt processing plant – pumping station ¾ hr, pumping station – car park ¾ hr; total time 2½ hr (12.2 km).

Ascent: None.

Grade: Easy walk along country trails and dyke paths.

Refreshments: Nothing available en route. Restaurants in Vila Real and Castro Marim.

Alternative: Specifically for walkers approaching by public transport, we recommend the following alternative: at the entrance gate to the nature reserve near the salt processing plant, turn right onto a narrow dirt road. After 800 m, turn right onto a tarmac road. Another 700 m further on, turn right along a tarmac road that merges from the left. Passing through olive groves, reach the centre of Castro Marim in not quite 2 km.

Tips: The nature reserve information centre in Castro Marim, the view from the battlements of the Moorish castle and the town of Vila Real de Santo António, with its many bustling shops, are also worth a visit.

Devotees of unusual birds will discover a paradise along this circular walk: flamingos, herons, storks and many species of smaller wetland birds. Whatever you do, be sure to bring along your binoculars!

Begin at the car park and continue west along the country lane. Soon close in on the Esteiro da Carrasqueira to the left. After not quite 1 km, the river bends left. Our return route will follow the adjacent dyke to bring us back to

Sunny trails through a birdwatcher's paradise.

this spot. Now, remain along the broad trail that swings right and steadily follows the salt flats. After another 1.3 km reach the **Esteiro da Leziria**. Swing left and keep to the narrow dirt road. This leads right then left skirting around a massive mound of salt and finally ends (we have now walked a total of 5 km) at the gate to the salt processing plant and the nature reserve which is privately-owned. Walking ahead into the nature reserve is permitted. With the salt processing plant on our left, keep straight ahead along the broad dirt trail in between the salt flats to the left and the little canal to the right. The trail swings left, then right. A good 1 km past the gate, swing left while taking in different views of Vila Real de Santo António, Castro Marim and of the shimmering Spanish enclave Ayamonte on the other side of the Rio Guadiana.

2½ km past the salt processing plant, reach the pumping station on the bank of the **Esteiro da Carrasqueira**. Here, turn left onto a path on top of the dyke alongside the river. Do not swing onto the broad trail on the other (left) side of the canal that keeps parallel to the watercourse – this returns to the salt processing plant! After a 2.5 km »dyke walk« the path merges into the approach trail. Turn right and in a few minutes return to the car park.

50 Rio Guadiana and Ribeira de Odeleite

A walk along the biggest and the prettiest rivers of the Algarve

Odeleite – Alcaria – Armoreira – Almada de Ouro – Foz de Odeleite – Odeleite

Starting point and destination: Odeleite, 45 m. Scheduled bus service to Vila Real de Santo António. By car: from the motorway IP 1 Faro – Spain, take the Castro Marim exit then along the N 122 for 14 km in the direction of Mértola. Parking possible at the village limits of Odeleite.
Walking times: Odeleite – Alcaria ½ hr, Alcaria – Armoreira ½ hr, Armoreira – Almada de Ouro ¼ hr, Almada de Ouro –

Foz de Odeleite 1¼ hr, Foz de Odeleite – Odeleite 1 h; total time 3½ hr (18.7 km).
Ascent: 175 m of ascents and descents.
Grade: Due to the length of the walk, a somewhat strenuous route along broad trails and narrow paths.
Refreshments: Bar/restaurants in Odeleite, Alcaria and Foz de Odeleite.
Tip: Take a boat-trip on the Rio Guadiana starting from Foz de Odeleite.

Of course, ocean galore – every Algarve tourist expects this – but rivers? Are there some of these, too? Are these bearers of fresh water really worth a visit, a walk? Indeed, every walker who forges into the »Far East« of the Algarve will find fascination in the river border Rio Guadiana and its tributaries: the beauty of the lush banks, the song of the nightingale, panoramic hills and pretty villages – the fruits of this walk as well.

Begin at the southern village limits of **Odeleite** and, in front of the café, descend a few metres along the village street only to turn immediately right onto a steep descending trail. This brings us rapidly to the Ribeira de

Odeleite at the foot of the dam wall. Test your balance along the stepping stones and cross over to the other side of the river. Turn left and ascend the broad trail. Enjoy lovely backward views of the pretty village garlanded with the greenery of citrus groves.

Soon enter open pine woods. Keep to the broadest trail ascending straight ahead, even when after 1.2 km a trail forks left and a junction must be crossed another 500 m later. Yet another 500 m on and the trail crosses the major road. To take a break, turn left here and walk for 200 m. In **Alcaria**, a simple bar/restaurant is waiting.

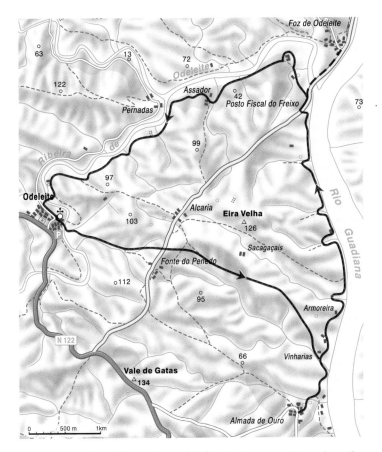

On the other side of the major road, following signs, continue along the broad trail. Only minor trails try to lure us to the right or left. Now we can relax during the descent and enjoy the ever greener and more fertile natural scenery.

After 2.5 km, reach the banks of the »big river«, the Rio Guadiana which flows from here for a very long distance acting as the border between Portugal and Spain. To the left, the few scattered houses of Armoreira – but a sign points to a trail on the right towards the lovely farming village of **Almada de**

Ouro. Along this trail and after 500 m bear left at a fork, cross over an easy ford and reach the village limits after a further kilometre. In front of the first houses, cross over a stream. In the village itself, a number of water sources offer healthy refreshment.

Refreshed and restored, we retrace our steps along the approach trail to return to Amoreira. Here, keep parallel to the riverside. After 500 m, pass by two farmsteads. Keep steady along the trail nearest the river until Foz de Odeleite. 500 m on, a trail merges from the left; keep bearing right. When the trail becomes less distinct after another 500 m, bear left and continue alongside the fields. Already 300 m later, meet up with another trail coming from the left and take this to the right. After another kilometre, continue along the trail, bearing left and ascending until it reaches a trail forking right and returning to the river. After another kilometre, this action is repeated.

When our trail ascends to the left, bear right then cross over a dry stream bed along a path. After 300 m meet up with the junction of a trail climbing down from a house above and to the left. Turn right onto this trail that leads directly to the banks of the river; turn left along a path. 1 km later, pass two houses to our left and then continue over fields to quickly reach the bridge

On the banks of the Ribeira de Odeleite.

spanning the **Ribeira de Odeleite**. On the other side of the river and about 300 m on, the first restaurant awaits at the village limits of **Foz de Odeleite** (the second is located on the other end at the northern village limits).

After retracing our steps and crossing back over the bridge, a signpost points out route ahead to Odeleite. The trail continues along the left bank of the river in the direction of our walk. At first, walk a broad trail to the right and then ascend left to a farmstead. Once there and after 500 m of walking, turn right.

Now the route keeps parallel to the banks of the Ribeira de Odeleite. Now relax and concentrate on the tranquil riverside, the green of the richly cultivated fields and vineyards, birdsong (we have also heard a nightingale here) and the hushed flow of the river.

After another 1½ km, pass through the hamlet Assador and, on the other side of the river at the confluence of the Ribeira da Foupana, pass the houses of the hamlet **Pernadas**.

Skirt around the ruins of a mill to our right and at a fork 1 km on, bear right. 800 m further on, cross a ford. Cross the river over a bridge then turn left onto a tarmac road. Continue by turning once to the right and then to the left through the village to return to the car park.

Other trails to be walked beyond the waters of the Baragem de Odeleite.

51 In the Mata Nacional das Terras da Ordem

Lush riverbanks, panoramic hills and unspoilt villages

Alamo – Foz de Odeleite

Starting point: Alamo, 15 m. Bus connection to Vila Real de Santo António. By car: from the IP 1 (Castro Marim exit) along the N 122 to the north for 12 km (towards Mértola) then turn right (signposted »Foz de Odeleite«). After 9 km, reach Alamo. Parking possible near the bus stop.
Destination: Foz de Odeleite, 15 m. Numerous daily bus connections to Vila Real. For the drive back, see above. 5 km of driving along a major road until reaching the junction of the EN 122.
Walking times: Alamo – Foz de Odeleite 1¾ hr (8.7 km).
Ascent: 170 m of ascents and descents.
Grade: Easy walk along broad trails.
Refreshments: Bar/restaurants in Foz de Odeleite.
Alternatives: If you wish to return from Foz de Odeleite to Alamo, you have a choice of alternative routes. During high season, you can use numerous daily bus connections or excursion boats along the Rio Guadiana. The shortest route on foot is along the major road that runs parallel to the river and reaches Alamo 4 km away. Time and again, you can switch away from the tarmac onto paths to the right running parallel and crossing over fields.

The prettiest route begins at the southern limits of Foz de Odeleite. From here, turn right and continue at first – in the direction of our walking – to the right of the Ribeira de Odeleite then 3 km on, to the right of the Ribeira da Foupana towards Tenencia. Once there, turn right onto the broad trail, cross over the *ribeira* then continue in an ascent for 2 km to reach a junction. From here, descend straight ahead to Alamo.

The region bordering Spain on the Rio Guadiana at the Algarve's easternmost end is still relatively unknown to tourists. Our short walk embraces the full beauty of this stretch of land nestled between two rivers.

Goats are our only companions.

Begin the walk only a few metres north of the bus stop by turning left onto a broad trail passing by the houses of the village of Alamo and ascending. After 150 m, our trail turns off to the left, crosses over a dry stream bed and then swings right ascending further on.

500 m on, at the upper village limits, a blue sign points the way to a trail climbing up to the left. After 600 m, ignore the first fork to the left. Not until 200 m later, turn left onto a broad trail whose course, descending at first, we can spot for a long distance in front of us. 800 m on, ignore a fork to our left and only

after another 700 m bear left at a fork and descend to a concrete bridge. Now an ascent begins, climbing gradually for almost 1.5 km until reaching a major junction. Here, continue the ascent by turning left. Now the most beautiful stretch of our walk begins – an almost 4 km long panoramic ridge trail that lets us stride high above the hilly countryside.

The trail forks after 500 m. Here, bear left and ignore all further forks by keeping to the steadily descending ridge trail. Soon reach the western village limits of **Foz de Odeleite**.

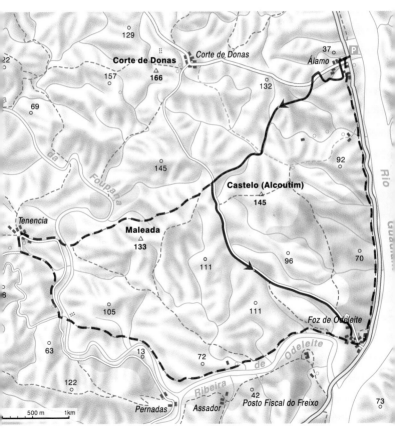

Index